Natalie

Only
Faith
REMAINS

A Journey of Hope, Love, **and**
Unbreakable Familly Bonds

Proofreading: Joanna Sosnowka Limitless Mind Publishing Ltd
Text composition: InkWander
Cover design: Malgorzata Sokolowska

ISBN: 9788396673985

LIMITLESS MIND
PUBLISHING

Limitless Mind Publishing Ltd
15 Carleton Road
Chichester
PO19 3NX
England
Tel. +44 7747761146
Email: office@limitlessmindpublishing.com

Dear Reader!

Find us on Facebook/Instagram:
limitless mind publishing

And visit our page on Amazon
by entering: limitless mind publishing into the search bar
or by scanning the QR code to see our other titles.

♥*We would greatly appreciate your opinion. It means a lot to us.*

For my daughter

From the Author

The useful and the useless must, like good and evil, go on together, and man must make his choice.

Mahatma Gandhi

Where does the boundary lie? When to say stop? Surrender or fight till the end? My wife and I had to answer these questions to ourselves at least a few times. This book contains a story about parenthood, where love for children takes precedence. And about how in one moment, a peaceful life turns into a race against time. When is the doctor right, and when is the parent right? Does a higher power exist? This is not a reading for the faint-hearted. Thanks to it, you will discover the true meaning of words: hospital, hospice, stress, tears, and helplessness. How strong must the will to survive be in order to deceive a certain death?

So let's start from the very beginning...

Table of Contents

Introduction

Life isn't about waiting for the storm to pass...It's about learning to dance in the rain.

Vivian Greene

I have always wanted to write a book, but I never imagined it would be this one. As a teenager, I knew that in the future, I would want to create a loving family. I planned to meet a beautiful girl, marry her, and have two wonderful children. However, I had to wait a long time for that one special person, and I searched in various ways. I had relationships with women whose way of being and priorities did not align with mine. I had the chance to meet both the overly jealous ones and those who prioritized a pack of cigarettes above all else. For many years, my life stood still.

After finishing school, I started working in a furniture store as an assistant for delivering furniture. After about a year, an opportunity arose for me to take a step further and make some changes in my life. Specifically, I was offered a job in the United Kingdom. I felt scared because I had no idea how it would all unfold. Many uncertainties tangled in my mind every time I went to bed, including the fact that I had never flown alone before. The closer the departure date approached, the more my hands trembled. It was a milestone towards changing my dull, everyday life.

I had no idea what to expect at the airport, and the lack of information only increased my stress. As I walked through the gates, a red alarm light flashed, further increasing my adrenaline. The reason for the situation was trivial. I had forgotten to put my glasses in the basket along with my phone and keys. Fortunately, after a moment, I was able to proceed. I glanced at the departure board, and to my annoyance, my flight was redirected to another terminal. The airport in Gdansk seemed really big to me, but fortunately, I didn't have to go far. After the final security checks, I boarded the plane, and as it began to taxi down the runway, I looked out the window, contemplating what the future would bring. A small suitcase and two hundred pounds in my pocket were all I had with me.

After arriving and getting accustomed to my rented room, I started to explore. However, I only had time for that when I had a day off from work. It varied. Due to my unpredictable schedule, sometimes it was a weekend, and other times it was a weekday. Everything was unfamiliar to me; I didn't know English well, and the left-hand traffic confused me. Initially, even looking in the right direction while crossing the street was a problem for me.

Everything I earned, I spent on paying for my apartment in Poland, food, and other necessary expenses for survival. I couldn't save anything. It wasn't something I had been eagerly waiting for, and slowly my enthusiasm was fading. I even had the thought of returning to my home country and starting anew, but one day everything changed. On a beautiful, sunny day, I met a girl with beautiful blonde hair. Right away, even before I knew her name, I knew I wanted to spend the rest of my life with her. After the initial moment of seeing her, I snapped out of the idyllic thought and came back to reality, telling myself that such scenarios only happen in fairy tales. However, I didn't give up on the idea. I introduced myself to her, and when she replied that her name was Eve, I immediately felt that I liked her name as well. We had coffee, ate delicious cake, and talked about various topics. When it got dark, she had to go back home. We exchanged numbers and arranged to meet again.

To visit her, I had to take a train and ride it through a few towns. I was completely stressed out, not even knowing where to buy a ticket because there was only a schedule on the platform. A foreign country and I didn't know the language well, and now I had to go to another unfamiliar city? I never expected to find myself in such a situation in my life. Finally, after a few adventures, when I got off at the destination station and saw Eve waiting for me, the stress left me. I smiled at her, and she reciprocated with the same gesture of gratitude.

I handed her a bouquet of roses, and then we went to explore the city. While sitting over coffee, I heard words from her that I will never forget for the rest of my life. She directly told me not to get my hopes up because she was returning permanently to Poland and didn't want to be involved with anyone at the moment. I left it without comment because it's hard to respond to such a definitive rejection on a first date. We explored the city a bit, and then I went back home. I thought it was the end of the adventure, but my subconscious prompted me to try calling again the next day. So I did. When I called, I asked if she would show me the part of the city we didn't get to see yesterday, and she agreed.

Despite her warning, I still decided to go see her. The first time, the second time, the third time, the fourth time. I knew she had a one-way ticket to Poland, had quit her job, was flying soon for her cousin's wedding, and wouldn't come back. That I would never see her again. I was devastated, unsure of what to do, but my concerns were dispelled by Eve herself! One day, she told me that she had reconsidered everything, bought a return ticket, revoked her resignation at work, and would let me know when she was coming back. It was a glimmer of hope for me. I felt like it was meant to be. And indeed, after a week in Poland, she returned, and deeply in love, we began our life together.

It was like a fairy tale. Shared travels, the same passions, and a similar outlook on the world. We managed to see quite a lot, met wonderful people, and tasted delicious food. However, something was missing; I felt a certain emptiness.

When we started getting to know each other, I told her about my dream of having two children. She was aware of it and accepted it, but we had to wait until she felt ready for such a step. For years, we didn't discuss the topic, but eventually, that changed too. Towards the end of 2015, Sebastian came into the world, and we felt happier than ever before. Step by step, we learned our new roles, showering our son with immense love. We made mistakes, but the challenges that arose were insignificant compared to the daily joy of being a family. A year later, we got married, baptized our little son, and moved from Wakefield to the smaller town of South Elmsall. We settled in a beautiful house with a garden and a wide, comfortable drivEvey for two cars. From our bedroom window, we could see a beautiful park created on the site of an old mine. There were nearly five kilometers of trails around, fresh air, and horses freely roaming near the park, which we could feed. Not everyone needs millions in their bank account to be happy; for me, my wife's smile and my son's laugh were enough.

After a few years, we decided to have another child. We were planning a trip to Sardinia, and two weeks before it, it turned out that Eve was pregnant. I was the happiest person on Earth! Another one of my dreams from my youth was about to come true. I was going to become a father for the second time! With this wonderful news, we flew to Sardinia to enjoy our vacation and savor delicious Italian cuisine.

After returning, we scheduled our first ultrasound appointment at the hospital in Wakefield to finally see our little one. We welcomed him with a smile on our faces. As we looked at the monitor, we saw him waving his little arms and legs around. The doctor confirmed that everything was fine with the baby, so we went back home and slowly started preparing for the upcoming Christmas holidays.

Like most expectant couples, we wondered about the gender of the baby and what name we would give him or her. We brainstormed, laughed, and simply enjoyed life.

One day, we received a letter with the date of our next ultrasound appointment at Pontefract Hospital, scheduled for January 19, 2019. I remember being surprised by the choice of the hospital because I had unpleasant memories associated with it. Last time, they struggled to draw blood for tests from our child, and eventually, they apologized and sent us back to the facility in Wakefield. We didn't feel like calling, arguing, and asking them to arrange the appointment at the place where our son was born. So, we left it as it was and went for the scheduled examination.

While waiting in the waiting room, we thought the procedure would go the same way as the previous examination, with the only difference being that we would find out the gender of the child. We entered the room twenty minutes late. Once again, we saw our little one on the monitor, kicking with their hands and feet just like before. We couldn't wait to hear whether it was a boy or a girl. Instead, the doctor asked my wife to lie on her side, which was strange to us because there had never been such a need before. A grave silence fell as the doctor stared at the monitor, examining the baby from every possible angle. We didn't know if we should speak first or if she would finally tell us what was going on. After a moment, she informed us that she suspected the last four vertebrae of the spine were not fully developed. It could indicate a spinal bifida, but further examinations with specialized equipment were scheduled at the children's hospital in Leeds next week. In the end, she revealed that it was a girl.

We were in complete shock; we had no idea what spinal bifida was. After the ultrasound, they took us to a separate room, where the nurses explained everything, repeatedly emphasizing that it was only a suspicion. There was an overwhelming amount of emotions, and Eve finally burst into tears. I tried to comfort her, saying that it wasn't certain, and after the examination next week, it might turn out to be a medical mistake because everyone makes errors.

We left the hospital and headed toward the parking lot. I held Sebastian's hand and looked at my wife, but her mind seemed to be somewhere else entirely. As I inserted the keys into the ignition, my hands were shaking. I kept telling myself that I needed to calm down and safely return home.

Diagnosis

Success is not final, failure is not fatal: it is the courage to continue that counts.

Winston Churchill

As we were driving back, I didn't know what to say. It was already dark, the road was winding, and I kept glancing at Eve, who seemed to be lost in her thoughts, far away. No matter what I said, I knew she wouldn't listen to me. When we finally arrived home, I tried not to dwell too much on the doctor's assumptions and instead focused on the joy of having a daughter. It was a dream of mine from my youth! I couldn't wait to share this news with our loved ones. I tried to comfort Eve, but it was in vain. I could see the sadness in her eyes all the time, and tears and stress filled every moment for her. I wanted her to be happy, to be able to enjoy the fact that we were going to have a girl, but my explanations did nothing to help.

Days passed, and in the meantime, we were reading articles on the internet about our doctor's assumptions. Well, my wife was reading, and I was trying to explain to her not to take to heart what was written there because, from my perspective, those were not reliable sources of information. I asked her to wait until the visit to draw any conclusions. She didn't listen. With each passing day, she delved deeper into pages describing spina bifida and how to cope with having a child with such a condition. The sadness in her eyes deepened. I was completely devastated. I wanted to help her, but none of my arguments seemed to resonate with her. Our three-year-old son could sense that something was going on, that his parents were arguing. He couldn't understand why Mom was crying. Looking back, I see how much he wanted attention. However, his attempts often ended with us raising our voices, which only brought forth more tears from him.

At work, I tried to diligently fulfill my duties, but my mind was at home. After a while, my behavior caught the attention of my manager, and he called me in for a brief conversation. When I explained everything to him, he told me to keep him updated on how the situation was progressing. He added that if I ever needed anything, I should come to him without hesitation.

I knew that I was entitled to fourteen days of paternity leave after the birth of the child. However, I wasn't sure if that time would be enough to properly settle everything. There was also the option of taking medical leave, but I was rather reluctant to consider it. Nevertheless, I tried to put it out of my mind.

Days passed, and the week seemed endless. Hour after hour, minute after minute, second after second... What will the doctors at the hospital in Leeds say? What will happen if the assumptions from the previous visit are confirmed? What should I do to take care of my family's well-being? Persistent questions kept popping up in my mind, and I couldn't find the answers. I told myself to take deep breaths, try to calm down, and simply wait for the next ultrasound.

Throughout this week, I can't count how many times I prepared a lemon balm infusion for Eve to calm her down. After all, she was pregnant, so stress was undesirable in her case. I did everything I could, even explaining that getting worked up could have a negative impact on the baby. All in vain. I had to wait until the end of the week when the atmosphere at home became unbearable.

The alarm clock rang at sunrise, and I got up feeling terribly exhausted. I couldn't sleep at night; I kept waking up from nightmares. It felt like a month had passed instead of a week. Finally, the day arrived when all doubts were supposed to be dispelled and forgotten, or so I thought. Because one always has to think positively!

We got into the car, I set up the GPS, and we set off on our way to the children's hospital in Leeds.

I was driving, glancing at Eve, just like the last time we were coming back from the hospital. However, this time I didn't say anything. I had to focus on the road because I really disliked driving in Leeds, especially in the city center. I made two lane mistakes, but we managed to find our way on the first attempt. Along the way, we encountered a small problem. The hospital parking lot was really small, and we couldn't find any available spots. So, we waited in line behind two cars, hoping that one of them would leave. We still had half an hour until our scheduled appointment, but the parking lot remained full. I asked my wife to take our son and go to the reception while I stayed behind. I wanted to be with her during the ultrasound, but it was more important not to be late for it.

I managed to park, and I had ten minutes left, although, in the end, we entered the examination room late.

Again, the same dark room. In the distance, the doctor sat clicking something on the computer, not even greeting us. The only person who greeted us was the technician who was going to perform the ultrasound. Specialized equipment was in the room where we were about to find out what our future would look like. Would everything be fine? Was the pregnancy really progressing abnormally? Another stress, another set of emotions that constantly accompanied us. Finally, after a few minutes, for the third time, we saw our little one on the monitor, squirming their legs and arms from left to right. It was a beautiful sight, but that wasn't why we came there.

The examination lasted over forty minutes, which was incredibly long for an ultrasound. Nobody said anything. Images appeared on the screen and quickly changed to the next ones. Finally, the doctor looked towards us and said that our child has a spinal bifida in the lumbar-sacral region. Our legs gave way beneath us. Suddenly, more questions came to mind, I can't even count how many we asked the doctor to find out as much as possible. From what we managed to learn at that time, our little daughter had the last four vertebrae underdeveloped, and such a pregnancy occurs once in every five hundred cases.

When the doctor saw my wife crying, he squatted beside her and began to explain the available options. First, he suggested that we could undergo surgery in London, but only up to the twenty-fourth week of pregnancy. As he described it, they would close the spinal bifida but would have to take the fetus (although I believe that the term "fetus" should be replaced with "baby" since it develops in the woman's body!) out of her belly, perform the operation, and then put our daughter back in. The aim of this surgery, besides closing the spinal bifida, was also to prevent complications that could arise later in the pregnancy. However, there was a significant catch: there was a thirty percent chance that the baby would be born prematurely, which could lead to further complications. Initially, my wife wanted to go to London and undergo the operation, but when she learned about the risk of prematurity, she decided against it.

Another proposal they gave us was to monitor the pregnancy until the very end, allowing the baby to develop naturally and giving birth to our daughter at the designated time in the Children's Hospital in Leeds.

The last option they presented to us was a termination of the pregnancy. Eve firmly responded that such an option was out of the question. She didn't want to terminate her own child just because something didn't go as planned on the ultrasound. After such an act, Eve wouldn't be the same person anymore. The guilt could destroy her mentally, and we still had our son who needed both parents!

After considering all the possible options, we chose the middle path. Continuing the pregnancy carried the risk of further complications, but it was a risk we had to take. We didn't have much choice, and this option seemed reasonable to us.

As we walked to the car, I saw the sad face of my wife all along, and it broke my heart. However, the only thing I could do was simply be there for her.

I set the GPS and we started our journey back home. As we entered the highway, I told Eve to remember that no matter how our daughter is born, we will accept her just the way she is. And we will show her how beautiful the world can be.

I couldn't do anything more. Throughout the rest of the journey back, only my favorite music played in the car. Sebastian fell asleep in his car seat, and Eve drifted away in her thoughts, staring out of the passenger window.

Flight to Poland

Most folks are about as happy as they make their minds up to be.

Abraham Lincoln

I brewed another cup of lemon balm tea for Eve. We sat in the kitchen and started to contemplate what to do next. We sat there for over half an hour, but nothing came to mind. This diagnosis put us in a hopeless situation. I told my wife to go to bed and try to relax a bit. She listened to me and didn't get up until morning when the emotions had subsided or quieted down. I had no idea how long this state of relative calmness would last.

We began consulting the entire situation with our loved ones. We tried to establish a step-by-step plan for further action.

Firstly, we knew the diagnosis. Secondly, we decided to continue with the pregnancy. We had also heard multiple times that even with specialized ultrasound equipment, there could be medical errors. There are real-life cases where a child was expected to be born with various genetic abnormalities, sometimes even severe ones, but ended up being born completely healthy.

So, there was a chance that there might have been an error in that hospital as well, and our little one could be healthy. We started searching for this hope on the Internet, going through the history of Polish specialists. We all searched wherever we could. We were in agreement that the more information we had, the better. After a few days of searching, we managed to find two respected specialists, one from Warsaw and another from Gdansk.

We purchased plane tickets to Gdansk in early February, right after my twenty-ninth birthday, and we flew there, temporarily leaving our rainy country for a while.

Upon arrival in Poland, we were greeted by a freezing, snowless winter and Eve's parents. We got into the car and started our journey to Puck, my wife's hometown. The trip went smoothly. We engaged in conversation on various topics to distract ourselves from constantly thinking about the pregnancy. The radio played Polish hits in the background, which I hadn't heard in a very long time.

When we arrived home, it was already very late, so we all went to sleep, leaving all the matters for the morning.

We woke up quite early. The climate change from British to Polish required us to adjust for a day or two. We walked up the stairs to the kitchen. I put the water on, and when the kettle whistled, releasing steam, I poured it over my favorite ground coffee. Eve and I sat in the living room, waiting for everyone to gather so we could discuss the purpose of our visit.

The most important aspect of this complicated situation was maintaining a positive mindset, as it was the only thing that gave us the strength to act. We held onto the hope that everything would turn out well, that all the words we heard from the doctors were just a mistake. After all, mistakes do happen!

We started to establish our plan of action. The first step was to travel to Warsaw, with a stop at a private clinic where Eve would undergo an examination. In this clinic, there was a chance for a less invasive surgery than the one proposed in London. It could be performed using the fetoscopic method, where the cleft could be closed without the need to remove the baby from the womb!

The next day, we had an appointment with a specialist in Gdansk.

All the appointments were scheduled a few days after our arrival to give us a brief respite from the situation and simply enjoy life. However, it didn't work out that way. There wasn't a single day when Eve didn't mention our child. The thoughts of our baby were constantly on her mind.

A few days before our trip to Warsaw, our son developed a fever and caught a cold. It was likely due to climate change. We agreed that Eve's mother would accompany her to the capital, while I stayed home with Sebastian to ensure his comfort and safety. He didn't get to see his grandfather and relatives every day. Two tickets for the express train were purchased, and in the early morning, two women with big hearts boarded the train and embarked on a four-hour journey.

Upon arrival, there was a six-kilometer distance from the main railway station to the clinic, which they decided to cover on foot due to having plenty of time. The concrete jungle, bustling city life, ongoing renovations, noise, traffic jams, and the rat race were the charms that they weren't particularly fond of.

Finally, amidst the sprawling construction sites, the girls arrived at the right address. They told me that they were pleasantly surprised by the personalized approach of the staff and the advanced equipment available at the clinic.

They spent maybe a few minutes, or perhaps longer, in the waiting room, but from what I know, Eve felt as if the time was much longer. She couldn't stay calm, and the stress intensified her impatience.

They entered the examination room. The young doctor greeted them and then proceeded to perform all the tests slowly and meticulously. Once again, it was the same procedure: ultrasound, the little one moving their arms and legs in all directions, dozens of images taken. All of this was done to obtain an accurate result and to confirm or challenge the diagnosis received in the United Kingdom.

The monitor has turned off once again, and the doctor's gaze turned towards Eve. The diagnosis was confirmed: the little one had a spinal cleft in the lumbar-sacral region. The last four vertebrae were not fully developed.

After the examination, the doctor had a conversation with Eve. He began by confirming the diagnosis and explaining that the fetoscopy procedure couldn't be performed due to a previa placenta. Then he started discussing the positives of the situation. Firstly, he pointed out that the baby was moving its legs, which was crucial in the case of a cleft in that particular area. Secondly, the cleft was not large, and the lower it was, the better the situation looked. Thirdly, he advised monitoring the pregnancy until the end, delivering the baby, and performing the surgery immediately after birth.

I was disappointed by the doctor's comment about me. When the girls mentioned that they wanted to share the information from the conversation with me, the doctor replied that if I were interested in knowing what was happening with the baby, I would have been there with them. I tried to rationalize it by considering that he was unaware of our other child's fever, who was also our whole world.

The visit came to an end.

I couldn't sleep; I waited for the arrival of my family and for them to tell me everything the doctor had said. I remember that when Eve returned, there was a wide, genuine smile on her face for the first time in a while. As soon as she entered the house, she went straight to Sebastian. She hugged him and instinctively checked his temperature. A few phone calls on the matter weren't enough for her, but it seemed natural to me. After the conversation with the doctor, she became more optimistic. We talked for a while and then went to sleep because Eve had an early wake-up call and another trip ahead. Since Sebastian still didn't feel well, I decided to stay with him once again.

Eve and her mother went to Gdansk while I was still asleep. I felt calm in the morning because what could possibly change within a day? I went upstairs and waited for the kettle to start whistling, so I could once again enjoy a delicious cup of freshly brewed coffee.

I spent the morning with my father-in-law, while also monitoring my son's condition. We had a chat, watched TV, and waited for the return of the family.

I sat on the corner sofa when I heard someone opening the door downstairs. After almost five minutes, I heard Eve climbing up the stairs. I was waiting for her with a smile because the doctor from Warsaw had allowed us to look at the pregnancy optimistically. Instead, at the doorway separating the hallway from the living room, I saw my wife, completely in tears, stressed, holding a cardboard folder from the clinic. I had no idea what was going on. Just yesterday, she came home with a smile on her face, and now she was crying again? I immediately asked her what happened. To which she replied, "Are you prepared for the worst? What kind of worst?" She told me that the doctor not only confirmed the previous diagnosis but also revealed to her that the baby has secondary hydrocephalus. She told her everything that could still happen, that the child might need a wheelchair, that there could be neurological problems, and so on.

I had to go on the defensive; I couldn't bear to see my wife cry again. I simply told her not to listen to that nonsense, to focus on the words she heard in Warsaw. I encouraged her to think positively and to push all the negatives out of her mind. However, it wasn't that simple, and once again, my arguments didn't have any effect. I felt defeated, desperately wanting to help her, but not knowing how to do it. My hands dropped, and I felt helpless once more.

We sat like that until evening. After long conversations with me and her mother, Eve started to calm down a bit.

I asked her if she had told me everything. In response, she told me that she had asked the doctor what she would do in her place. She was told that the doctor would terminate the pregnancy. And she proposed it to her. I was shocked. How could someone say such a thing to a patient? How could they encourage someone to terminate, or rather, to kill a living, innocent being? Did these people have no empathy? No conscience? It seemed easier for them to avoid the problem altogether. I stuck to my belief of listening to what was said in the capital. I repeated it to her once again and went to sleep. I had had enough of sadness, worries, and tears.

We stayed in Poland for a few more days. The atmosphere became somewhat lighter, although there wasn't a day that we didn't think about our baby even for a moment.

Finally, the day of our return home arrived. We packed our bags and set off on a journey to the airport, and then we flew to Doncaster in the United Kingdom. When we landed, it was already dark and raining. We waited for a while until the parking company brought our car, and then we headed back home.

Waiting for the next visit

*Never give up on a dream just because of the time it will take to ac-
complish it. C e time will pass anyway.*

Earl Nightingale

After returning, nothing was the same anymore. Since we heard the
confirmation of the diagnosis, our lives turned upside down. We were
devastated, and the awareness of our little daughter's condition and potential neurological complications only made matters worse. Day after
day went by. We tried to live normally, think positively, and speak to
our baby as often as possible. However, the thought of when the next
appointment would come was always in the back of our minds because
we knew the pregnancy had to be monitored. The only mystery was
how many more tests awaited us.

After almost two weeks, the anticipated correspondence arrived. I
immediately opened it, glanced at the date of the next visit, and the
name of the hospital we were supposed to go to. The letter stated that
we should go to the hospital in Wakefield in three weeks, not Leeds,
where we were last time. It surprised us a bit because we thought the
pregnancy would be monitored weekly.

We had to arm ourselves with patience. In the meantime, my mom
flew over to help us out with Sebastian. She happened to be with us on
the day of our scheduled ultrasound appointment. Thanks to her presence, we could calmly talk to the doctors, while my mom took care of
our son at home during that time.

The next visit was delayed, but we eventually entered the room.
We knew what awaited us, with the only difference being that there
were more doctors present. The only thing I enjoyed about these examinations was the fact that each time we could see our little baby. It
was incredible to witness the dormant energy within her, as she wrig-

gled her limbs in all directions, and especially how she turned her head towards us.

When the people in white coats finished their examinations, everyone's gaze turned toward us. Based on previous experiences, I inferred that it didn't bode well. So, I asked straight to the point, "What is it about this time?"

The skin of the child in the cleft area was open but covered with a membrane. They told us that there was a possibility of the membrane rupturing, which could allow cerebrospinal fluid to leak out, carrying a significant risk of further complications.

Once again, my hair stood on end, and a shiver ran down my spine. With each new piece of information from the examination, we discovered more terrifying things. Our well-being plummeted to a very low level.

With the new information in hand, we returned home feeling utterly drained. We had no strength left. After a brief greeting, Sebastian went back to playing in the living room with his grandmother. Even enjoying ice cream while watching our favorite TV show didn't bring us any pleasure. It was impossible to drown out all the information we had received in any way.

Despite his young age, our son could sense that his parents were sad, but he didn't know the reason behind it. It was only logical since he was just three years old. Like any child at that age, he wanted to grab our attention, so he started misbehaving to get our focus.

The following day, we had to sit down and establish a plan of action because the situation had become too serious. We talked from noon until evening, thoroughly analyzing the entire situation. After careful consideration, we decided to continue living our lives as we did before the pregnancy. The sole priority was to dedicate time to our son because we had neglected that aspect, which shouldn't have happened. Despite all the discouraging words we had heard thus far, we didn't lose hope. Three more ultrasounds awaited us, this time at the children's hospital in Leeds, as that was where the delivery was scheduled to take place.

The days passed by, and life continued to unfold. We started gaining some distance from the situation and devoted more free time to our son. My wife took care of herself consistently, often engaging in conversations with our little daughter. I, on the other hand, tried to be a bit silly to make those moments primarily fun-filled. Every way to improve the overall mood for all of us was priceless.

We decided to take the train for the next visit. I didn't want to experience the stress of searching for a parking spot again, especially before such an important ultrasound appointment.

The check-up went well. Fortunately, no further complications were detected, and the membrane did not rupture, which was our biggest concern.

We had no choice but to wait for the next letter. Fortunately, it arrived after a few days, and the information it contained indicated another ultrasound in three weeks' time.

We continued with our daily routine, which was now enriched by the intense movements of the little one inside Eve's belly. I remember that whenever I placed my ear against her stomach, I would often receive a strong, energetic kick.

The following weeks went by quickly, and when the time came, we went for the visit using the train, just like the last time. Our son was incredibly excited because trains were something that fascinated him.

It was our last ultrasound, and the only thing that mattered to us was receiving confirmation of no further complications. Thank God, nothing else happened. The doctors reminded us that this was the final check-up, and until delivery, there was no need for us to come again unless any concerns arose.

With less than two months left until the due date, we had to make arrangements for Sebastian when the delivery day arrived. We needed someone to take care of him so that both of us could go to the hospital. After discussing it together, we decided that I would utilize the remaining days of my leave from work to fly with our son to Poland, to Eve's parents. I would stay there for a few days to let Sebastian acclimate, and then I would return to Eve on my own.

The entire plan seemed like a fairytale, but in reality, it was anything but. We left on the second of June, and I returned on the fifth. Eve's due date was set for the seventh of June, and the risk of it starting earlier was significant. I was afraid that I wouldn't make it in time, but we couldn't leave our son behind without any acclimatization. So, I prayed for everything to go according to plan. However, I didn't forget to take precautions for Eve, just in case. We informed our neighbors about the situation and prepared taxi numbers. Calling an ambulance wouldn't make sense for a simple reason. The ambulance driver would be obligated to take the patient to the nearest facility in the region, which, in this case, would be Pontefract Hospital. It was the last place we wanted to end up.

On one hand, I was panicking because I had to leave my pregnant wife alone at home just a few days before her due date. On the other hand, the idea of flying alone with our son for the first time, without Mom, on a little male adventure, excited me.

Before leaving for the airport, I pressed my lips against Eve's belly and told our daughter to wait for me. I kissed her little bump, received a goodbye kick to the teeth, put the backpack in the trunk, and then we set off to the airport with our son.

Father and Son

Humanity is about caring for your family and the ability to make sacrifices for others.

Magic Johnson

It was a really strange feeling. We were flying to Poland with my son, without his mom who had always accompanied us before. At first, I thought Sebastian would be asking about Eve, but luckily we managed to avoid that. We arrived at the airport a little early. The last thing I wanted was to be anywhere at the last minute. I never liked being late, although a few times I had to run for a train or bus, and I know how stressful it can be. While waiting for our flight, we stopped by Subway to grab a sandwich. Once we finished eating and paid a fortune for it, we went to watch the departing and landing planes. So our time passed by observing these huge machines, which brought a lot of visual joy to my child. The only concern was the late flight time from Doncaster to Gdansk. I was worried if our son would even go to sleep. It turned out that I was unnecessarily worried. After boarding, we got on the plane and managed to sit by the window, and as soon as the plane reached the appropriate altitude, Sebastian fell asleep. I suspect that in another case, he would want to explore every corner of the cabin.

He woke up just before landing. The customs clearance went smoothly. I called my in-laws, and shortly after, they arrived to pick us up.

Just like last time, the Polish radio was playing in the car, and the journey went smoothly.

In the morning, we were greeted by beautiful sunshine in the clear sky. After breakfast, I video-called Eve to ask how she was feeling. Thankfully, everything was going according to plan, and the baby wasn't in a hurry to come into the world. I spoke with her for only a short while because lunch was about to be served. The food was delicious, as always. I took a few minutes to rest, while Sebastian stayed with his grandmother, and then my sister-in-law and I went for a run. We started from Puck, ran through Połczyno, then Brudzewo, Celbowo, and finally back to Puck. Together, we covered over twelve kilometers in one hour and thirteen minutes. Not bad, although we've had better results before. It was only after the run that I realized eating meatballs before training wasn't the best idea. On top of that, I wanted to break into my new shoes. Unfortunately, I forgot to put plasters on my feet, and the run resulted in some minor blisters on my heels.

I was preparing for the Spartan Race, which was scheduled to take place in July. There were two distances, one on Saturday and the other on Sunday. It was a challenge for me, and despite the situation with my daughter, I didn't want to give up on it. It was important for me to maintain a balance, both mentally and physically.

We returned home, and I was curious to see how our little one was behaving with their grandmother. As it turned out, they were well-behaved and spent the entire time in the backyard, playing in a small pool. I particularly enjoyed watching how they held the hose and dropped toys into the pool while being fascinated by the water flowing onto the grass.

As the day came to an end, we decided to extend it a little bit and organized a barbecue in the garden while Sebastian was sleeping. Holding a bottle of beer in my hand, I couldn't help but constantly think about how my wife was managing on her own at home and whether the baby might decide to come earlier. Despite trying to keep my emotions in check, my mind was still filled with worries.

In the evening, I called Eve again. She reassured me that the baby wasn't in a hurry to arrive. With that information, I could go to sleep feeling relieved.

Another day has come. June was undoubtedly very hot. By nine o'clock in the morning, you could already feel the temperature rising. It promised to be a beautiful morning.

We went for a quick shopping trip and then stopped by an ice cream parlor to give our little one a small surprise. He loved sweet treats, especially ice cream, so the outing was a delightful experience for him.

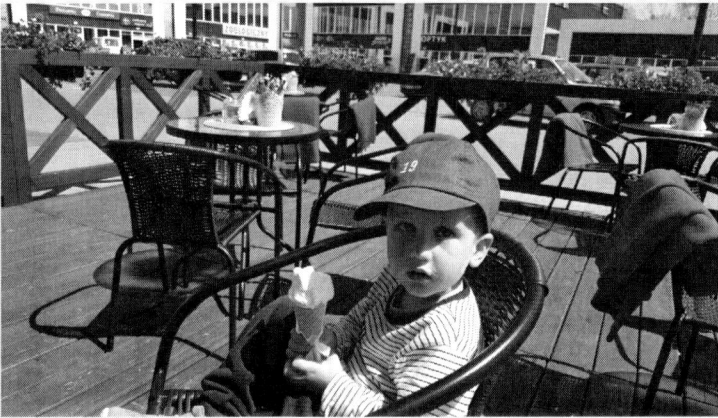

Going out with my son for ice cream on a hot day was a delightful experience

Upon returning home, I had to disappear again to allow Sebastian to get accustomed to the situation that Dad wasn't around. Each time, he would hear that Dad went to work. The most common reason for leaving the house was for training sessions. I enrolled in a few gym sessions to continue working on my fitness and prepare myself for the upcoming obstacle race. The gym had a wide range of equipment that helped me in my preparations.

Preparations for the Spartan Race

I approached all the training intensively but with a greater focus on endurance exercises rather than strength training. With each passing day, my fitness level improved significantly.

Every time I came back home, it turned out that my three-year-old was doing amazingly well. He didn't cry at all. Despite the absence of his dad, it didn't bother him. Everyone was most concerned that the child would cry for me.

I spent the last two days in Poland peacefully, calling Eve every day to inquire about the situation. I spent time with my son and family. I didn't visit anyone because I had no head or time for it at all.

This very short trip was wonderful because it allowed me not only to spend time with my loved ones but also to gain some perspective on reality. However, I had to return to my wife.

On the evening of June 5th, I went to the airport in Gdansk for my return flight. I boarded the plane and set off on the journey.

I landed in Doncaster and felt the cold, so different from the summer weather in Poland. It was June, but there wasn't any nice weather in England at that time. I picked up my car and drove home. Raindrops lazily slid down the car windows, and due to the late hour, darkness surrounded me. I drove cautiously, thinking about what was happening with my son in Poland and with Eve at home. I had to focus on driving, but these thoughts troubled me. I wanted to be home as quickly as possible, but the motorway with the exit to my town was closed. The sign "roadworks" forced me to change plans and take a route through the city. Despite the late hour, I got stuck in traffic, and I arrived home two hours later than planned.

I greeted my wife and the little one, and then we went to sleep. In the morning, I told them about how my stay in our home country went. In the meantime, I also learned that my mother would come to us on Saturday after the planned delivery, which brought me great relief. Help in such moments is worth its weight in gold.

Hours and days passed until the most important day finally arrived, the day of resolution that we had been eagerly awaiting for so long.

Birth

Life is not the way it's supposed to be, it's the way it is. C e way you cope with it is what makes the difference.

Virginia Satir

We hardly slept the whole night. In the morning, we were supposed to call the hospital in Leeds and find out what time we should arrive for the induction. The bag had been packed two days before the due date, and as it turned out on the phone, it still had to stay at home for a while. We were informed by the lady at the office that there were no available beds, so we had to call every day to find out if any bed became available.

We were completely dissatisfied with this. First, they told us to come for the induction on the 7th of June because the delivery was supposed to be monitored, specialists were supposed to be present, and the baby was supposed to be taken immediately after birth. And then suddenly we find out that there are no available spots! It's a total absurdity!

We couldn't do anything about it, even though we believed that the facility's organization was at zero level. All we could do was wait until Saturday and make another phone call then.

In the early morning, we called again, and once again, there was no space available for us! The lady on the phone told us to call when the contractions start.

A few hours after making the call, my mother arrived at our place. We sat together until the evening, talking, or rather speculating, about how our daughter would look and whether she would have as much hair as her brother did when he was born. We reminisced, laughed, and then went to sleep.

Sunday arrived. It was 6 o'clock in the morning when my wife woke me up and said that we were going to the hospital because it had begun.

We all got into the car, and after thirty-five minutes, we arrived at the hospital. Fortunately, I managed to stay calm, as otherwise, we would have had to walk the distance. Eve got out of the car and went into the hospital a little faster, while my mother and I waited for a parking spot. After five minutes, we rushed to the admissions ward. We went up to the upper floor, and Eve went in for the routine examinations, which lasted about three hours. When the doctors determined that it was time for delivery, we entered the room where everything was going to happen. My mother sat in the waiting area, but to her surprise, after a few minutes, a midwife approached her and asked if she would like to come with us into the delivery room. She agreed, still astonished, as she never expected to be present at the birth of her own granddaughter.

A few hours passed, and Natalie was born into the world. It was Sunday, the 9th of June, two days past the due date. She weighed three thousand four hundred fifty grams, a bundle of happiness. Unfortunately, we couldn't enjoy her presence for long. She had to be taken away as quickly as possible. There was an open wound on her back, just above her buttocks, a small one. It looked as if she had cut herself on the edge of a table. The nurses wrapped the area with cling film because clear fluid started seeping from the wound.

The midwife attending the delivery was impressed. She said that in her career, she had never encountered a woman who remained so composed and didn't emit any screams. Eve was so focused on the swift birth of her daughter that she solely concentrated on the process, without making any louder sounds.

The baby was taken from the room, and postpartum procedures were carried out in the ward. Later, when Eve had rested, they showed her which bed had been prepared for her and directed her to which department she should go.

We escorted her to the designated place, said our goodbyes, and then my mother and I returned home.

The next day, we took the train to visit our girls, leaving the car in the parking lot beneath the platform. We brought Eve some groceries that she had forgotten to pack in her bag earlier, as well as two hundred panoramic crosswords.

While staying at the hospital, we found out that the operation had been postponed until Tuesday because there were no specialists available at that time to perform the spinal closure. We stayed with Eve as long as we could, but it wasn't for very long. In the evening, we picked up Eve's mother and Sebastian from the airport. We said our goodbyes, reassuring them not to worry. Unfortunately, it was evident that my wife was experiencing postpartum shock.

Once again, nothing sat right with me. Dozens of questions started racing through my mind. Why didn't the delivery happen on the scheduled date? Why was such an important operation delayed by two whole days? And why was my wife experiencing postpartum shock just like with our first child? I couldn't find answers to all these questions.

We set off to the airport to pick up the remaining family members. In the evening, after Sebastian went to sleep, we decided to celebrate the birth of Natalie with a bottle of Martini.

On Tuesday morning, my mother drove to the airport in a rented car to have extra time before her afternoon departure to Belfast, where she lived. At the same time, we were on our way to Leeds to meet Eve as quickly as possible. The presence of her mother should greatly improve her well-being. We arrived at the hospital, went up to the third floor, and headed to Eve's room. The expression on my wife's face upon seeing her mother was priceless. She was overjoyed and told us that Natalie had been taken for spinal closure surgery an hour ago, but the doctors couldn't estimate how long it would take. Sebastian started getting bored, so we went to the playroom on the same floor, where we found plenty of toys and two sofas. Our son began playing, and we had some time for a peaceful conversation. After a while, Eve saw through the partially opened door the doctors wheeling a portable incubator in which she glimpsed our baby girl. She hurried to the reception to inquire about everything. We couldn't see her right away. We had to wait until they transferred her to a regular incubator. We entered a colorful room with nine beds for infants after surgery. All the beds were occupied. It was then, being in such a place for the first time, that I realized these kinds of things exist, that human tragedies are among us. In my search for a bed with Natalie, whether I wanted to or not, I looked at other children and their parents, mostly with sad expressions or tears in their eyes.

Finally, Natalie came into our sight. She was sleeping, but that was good because sleep heals. We all approached the incubator to get a closer look at her. The hospital regulations allowed only two people to be present at the incubator, so I stepped aside for my mother-in-law. I knew I would have plenty of time to enjoy my daughter. We took turns going into the room, sometimes it was me, and other times it was Eve's mother.

We knew that Eve was overwhelmed by the situation. She started asking other parents about their children's conditions, which only made her feel worse. So we decided to persuade her to come back home with us that day. We reassured her that Natalie was under the care of doctors and that nothing would happen to her there. We spent some more time with our daughter and then went to pack our things. Before heading to the platform, we got hungry and stopped by our favorite Thai restaurant. When we returned home, Eve regained some color in her face, and her eyes weren't as sad anymore.

The next morning, we went to see our little one. To our surprise, she was lying on her back, which she shouldn't have been doing. After all, she had just undergone surgery, and it was important for her to lie on her stomach to aid in the healing process. Upon our arrival and explanation to the doctors that the baby was in the wrong position, they turned her onto her stomach. The entire postoperative wound was covered with honey dressing, so we couldn't see if anything had accidentally been damaged. We were also informed that they wouldn't be able to change her position frequently, for now, considering the wound. We desperately wanted to avoid pressure sores, so we were concerned about the situation. We spent some time in the room with the nine beds, waiting for Eve to express milk because breastfeeding wasn't possible, and then we went to the playroom.

My mother-in-law called her son and asked him to book her return ticket home for the following day. She stated that we would manage and requested us to keep her informed, especially when Natalie is discharged from the hospital. The next day, we went to drop off my mother-in-law at the airport.

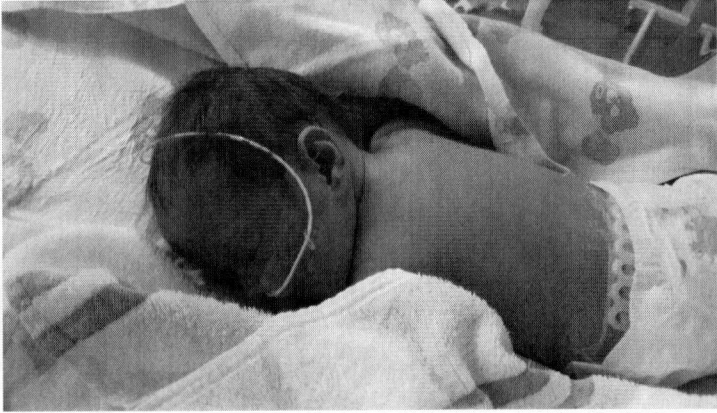

Natalie, after the surgery, had her cleft closed and secured with a honey dressing

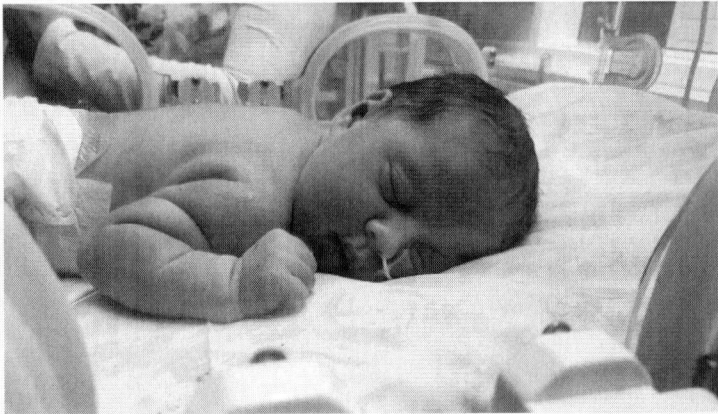

The first meeting with my daughter after the surgery

Further complications

C ere is only one thing that makes a dream impossible to achieve: the fear of failure.

Paulo Coelho

I don't remember the last time I slept so well. I woke up in the morning, even before Eve and Sebastian, and went downstairs to prepare breakfast. After about thirty minutes, everyone was up, and the kitchen was filled with the smell of scrambled eggs with bacon and coffee. The meal had to be substantial because we had a whole day ahead of us outside of the home.

We were about to leave when suddenly the phone rang from the hospital. It turned out that Natalie's head had started to enlarge, and it was necessary to insert a shunt. Hydrocephalus was developing, and the doctors had to react urgently, pleading with us over the phone for consent to the surgery. We had no choice but to agree to it. To make matters worse, on the same day, when we were already on the platform, feeling stressed, the train was canceled, and we had to wait for over an hour until the next one arrived. The reason for this unfortunate situation was a malfunctioning traffic signal that paralyzed the entire railway system. Sitting on the delayed train, our thoughts were only about our child, as this was not part of the plan. The cleft was supposed to be closed, and Natalie was supposed to be discharged home, but now more complications were arising. After getting off the platform, we quickly caught bus number five and went to the facility. Upon reaching Floor C, we couldn't find our daughter, and they explained to us that she had been taken to the operating block. We waited in vain because we didn't know how long the surgery would take. So we went to the cafeteria to have something to eat, even though we didn't want to due to the high prices. For a not very substantial lunch for three people, we had to pay over fifteen pounds! Once our money was depleted, we went to the playroom to keep Sebastian entertained. We waited, constantly glancing at the clock. Finally, after several hours, they brought Natalie back to the room where the children who had undergone surgery were lying. Approaching her incubator, I burst into tears, as did Eve. There was visible hairless skin and a visible stitch next to her little ear, with a slight bulge underneath. But that wasn't all. A stitch had also been placed on her abdomen because the shunt led from her head and ended somewhere in her abdomen. All this was done so that cerebrospinal fluid could flow normally instead of accumulating in the child's brain. Poor Natalie. She had only recently been born, and she had already undergone two major surgeries. In addition to that, she couldn't lie on her back like a healthy baby but had to be on her stomach all the time. She couldn't breastfeed but had to rely on bottle feeding. However, one positive thing in all of this was that the baby was receiving the mother's milk, which was expressed daily. A sufficient supply of breast milk was successfully collected and stored in the freezer in the same ward. Eve was constantly stressed, which caused her milk supply to decrease. Nevertheless, she never gave up to ensure Natalie had consistent access to breast milk. We sat by her incubator while our son watched cartoons on the phone. If we wanted some time for contemplation, connecting to the hospital's free Wi-Fi and letting him watch cartoons was our only option. I sat there with a sad expression, gazing at the stitch on my daughter's head, when suddenly the voice of a man in a white coat caught my attention. It was a neurologist accompanied by an assistant. We stood up to listen to what they had to say, and they had a lot to tell us. They had to explain everything in detail. After some time, we calmed down as they explained everything to us and informed us that the surgery was successful. Neurologists would be observing Natalie, though not necessarily the ones we were talking to. They would come daily to measure her head circumference, check if the hydrocephalus was receding, and ensure the shunt was functioning properly. After the surgery, I remembered what Professor from Gdansk had said about secondary hydrocephalus and potential complications besides the spinal cleft, but clinging to positive thinking, I simply ignored it. Life showed that I was wrong. Positive thinking is one thing, but being aware of what could happen, even if it's not certain, is another.

Natalie practically slept the entire time after another surgery, but that's alright. Sleep is good for everything, especially for such a young child. I lost count of how many times we left the hospital, saying good-bye to our daughter and telling her that we would come back tomorrow. So we returned home, had some lemon balm tea, and went to sleep. That day was exhausting. We wanted to get some rest and go back to the hospital in the morning, hoping that the train wouldn't be delayed or canceled due to malfunctioning traffic lights. Fortunately, our son had time off from preschool during that period, so we could take him with us. The main reason was that I didn't want to leave my wife alone with everything. I wanted to be with her all the time. During that time, we argued frequently, but supporting her remained my priority. The whole situation began to overwhelm us; everything was going in the opposite direction of how it should be.

The next day we arrived in Leeds and decided to walk to the hospital. Even on a weekday, the city was bustling with people, and there were homeless individuals sitting on almost every corner, often with dogs, begging for small change. The number of people sitting on the streets was frightening. Most of them were young, but occasionally we could also see elderly individuals. The walk from the platform to the hospital took about fifteen minutes. Since we were walking with our three-year-old, the journey took a bit longer. If Sebastian indicated that he was hungry, we would enter a shop with ready-made sandwiches and buy him a ham and cheese baguette, asking the friendly staff to toast it so that it wouldn't be cold. With that, the walk to the hospital took us about half an hour. As we crossed the bridge over the expressway, passing by a homeless old man with a long gray beard and his dog, and a tattered tent, and then turning into a small alley on the right, we arrived at the hospital. Upon reaching the third floor, we waited for someone from the reception to open the doors for us. We entered the room, and our little one was asleep. Eve had already expressed her milk, and after a while, neurologists entered the ward to perform routine examinations. They took out a notepad, a pen, and a large measuring tape, which they wrapped around Natalie's head. After a few measurements and notes, they began talking to us. Fortunately, they informed us that the shunt was functioning properly, and the circumference of our child's head was decreasing. We breathed a sigh of relief upon hearing those words. The last thing we needed was for hydrocephalus to worsen. We asked the neurologists about everything that came to our minds. We were particularly interested in how to manage when our child would be discharged, how to recognize if something was wrong and the shunt wasn't working correctly, what the first symptoms were, how to react, and many other questions. In order to have a calm conversation with the doctors, we had to once again let our older child watch cartoons. We didn't want to do it too often, but the situation forced us to. While Sebastian was engrossed in the screen of his phone, we discussed the shunt and hydrocephalus. After the conversation, we tried to remember everything, but it was difficult because the stress accompanying us at the time prevented logical thinking. Some time passed, the neurologists left the room, and we had a little time to sit with our daughter. Tears were streaming down our faces, and we also had headaches and stuffy noses. We felt drained. Through tear-filled eyes, we could see the looks from other parents directed toward us. Surely they had cried many times themselves and knew exactly how we were feeling at that moment. My heart broke as I saw all those children. They had only recently been born, yet they had already been through so much.

Returning from the restroom, where I went to wash my face from tears, I realized that there was no point in staying at the hospital any longer today. It was terribly depressing for me, and I assume for my wife as well. So we went outside, leaving behind that cursed building. We also walked back to the platform, checked which station our train was departing from, and went to the platform. The train was very crowded; we must have caught it during the worst time, as most passengers were probably returning from work. I didn't blame them at all for commuting by train to Leeds and back. Driving and finding a parking spot would have been quite a challenge.

Sebastian really enjoyed traveling by train. If he could, he wouldn't get off it at all. We didn't have anyone to leave him with, so we took him with us every time we went to Natalie's.

My paternity leave after Natalie's birth passed by very quickly, and I was forced to take medical leave. Now, it has been three weeks, but the doctor told me that I would be able to extend it if necessary. So, I brought a small piece of paper with a stamp to work and explained that I would keep them updated on the situation. At that moment, I couldn't predict how long all of this would last.

Day after day passed, and we eagerly awaited her discharge from the hospital. They had previously said it depended on how quickly the wound would heal, but they estimated it could take anywhere from two to three weeks. After the valve replacement, this period could be extended by another two weeks. It was definitely not the news we wanted to hear, but we had to come to terms with it. We didn't have any other choice.

A Breather

You can't have a better tomorrow if you are thinking about yesterday all the time.

Charles F. Kettering

Through all this fuss about our daughter, we almost forgot about our son's needs. The daily commute to the hospital was tiring not only for us but also for him. July was approaching, along with warm, sunny days. That's why we decided to let Sebastian try his hand at his first obstacle race. Every time we went to my competitions, he absolutely loved it. He enjoyed cheering and, if he could, he would have joined the starting line himself. However, his age didn't allow him to do that back then. We searched the internet a bit and found an obstacle race for children where a three-and-a-half-year-old can already participate with a guardian! We purchased a ticket for the sixth of July. The start was in the first wave at ten o'clock, covering a distance of three kilometers. The distance was suitable as we wanted to see if he could run that much and how he would handle the obstacles under my supervision.

We started training. Sebastian had been running with me before but without obstacles. One day, after having breakfast and taking a one-hour break, we went to the park behind our house to train. We combined running with obstacles, which had an amazing effect. Every time we went out for training, I told him that once he completed his first race, he would receive a medal after crossing the finish line. We trained almost every day after returning from the hospital. The only exception was rainy days when we would watch Spartan Race videos on online TV, lay out a mat, and exercise at home.

Days went by, and we stuck to our plan. Sebastian couldn't wait for Saturday; he was so eager to run. In the evening, he didn't even want to go to sleep. He kept holding onto his backpack, where he had packed his clothes and running shoes, and he wanted to go to the car, even though it was already dark and past 9 p.m. After some negotiation, he finally went to bed, but he woke up before everyone else, at five in the morning. My alarm was set for six, but there was no chance of sleeping anymore. So, I got up with him, and we went to prepare breakfast before his mom's alarm went off.

After eating, we got into the car. I set the GPS, and we embarked on a two-hour journey. Upon arrival, we went to the registration tent. I saw plenty of older kids, but not many as little as our son. After registering, we changed into our club uniforms and headed to the starting line. A man standing on a haystack began leading a warm-up session, during which we did push-ups, jumping jacks, squats, and many other exercises. The warm-up lasted about five minutes, and I saw a smile on our son's face. He was incredibly happy, and when the starting signal was given, he dashed ahead without waiting for me. I quickly caught up with him because I knew that if I disappeared from his sight for too long, he would start crying. So, we began our first-ever obstacle race together. We encountered obstacles that Sebastian could tackle on his own, like tunnels made of hay bales or climbing over hay bales. There were also obstacles where he needed my help, such as climbing over tires or traversing a massive inflatable cushion wrapped in a fishing net. We had a great time, overcoming a distance of over three kilometers filled with uneven terrain, streams, and other fantastic obstacles. Even though we were running, I couldn't stop thinking about Natalie. My mind was cluttered with questions like what is she doing now? How is the hospital staff taking care of her? Is her head shrinking? Is the wound from the back surgery healing properly? Is the valve working correctly? I truly wanted to focus only on the race, my son, and my wife during that time, but I couldn't do it. I kept thinking about her and that damn hospital.

We were approaching the finish line, and for a moment, I managed to forget about everything and enjoy the accomplishment of completing the race. It was definitely not our last race like this. We got back into the car and started our journey back on the country road. It was no surprise that after such exertion, Sebastian quickly fell asleep in the car.

We had a two-hour journey ahead of us, with a short break for food, and then the rest of the day was dedicated to resting because we had to go to the hospital in the morning. Exhausted after the entire day, we returned home and went to sleep.

The next day, we were supposed to go to the hospital again, but my body clearly signaled that we should take a break. We were exhausted, so we decided to have a day off from the facility on Sunday. My wife took only her phone and made a call to inquire about how our child was feeling, whether the neurologists had measured her head circumference, and asked a few more questions. After pressing the red button to end the call, she told me that everything was fine with our little one. It was a relief to hear that things were progressing well, and that our daughter would be with us at home soon. For the rest of the day, we did nothing, and Sebastian watched cartoons because we didn't even have the energy to play with him.

Monday arrived, and we fell into our familiar routine. Breakfast, train, hospital, and lunch in town because we had neither the strength nor the desire to cook at home. After arriving at our daughter's side, we had a moment to talk to the doctors. Natalie's surgical wound was healing very slowly. She had been in the hospital for a month already, and it didn't seem like she would be discharged anytime soon. We held onto the hope that we would be able to bring her home with us before my obstacle race trips. Unfortunately, there was no talk of her being discharged from the hospital, and her knee started turning red because the doctors didn't change her position frequently enough during our absence. Another week went by. Day after day, we visited our little one. The truth was that we had to monitor everything because we didn't know how much attention the staff gave to the patient when we weren't there. On our way back home, while staring out of the train window, I couldn't help but think about her, lying there all alone in that damn hospital.

One of Sebastian's favorite obstacles was crawling through a tunnel

When we went to the hospital again on Friday morning, we didn't expect anything new. We informed the doctors once again that we wouldn't be in the hospital over the weekend and asked if they could take care of our little one. We requested them to change her position more frequently, apply ointment to her knee, and, whenever possible, give her hugs to make her feel the presence of other people. They said they would do so and wished us a pleasant weekend. I was very skeptical about what they said. Many times they made promises but didn't follow through. I said goodbye to Natalie, giving her a gentle kiss and telling her to stay strong during the time we wouldn't be there. With tears in my eyes, I left the hospital, looking at the windows on the gray walls of the building. Every time I left the facility, I automatically felt sad. We didn't want to leave her there, but we had no other choice. The pain I felt during that time was indescribable. I never imagined that one could miss their own child so much. We turned towards the bridge over the expressway, passed the same homeless man again, and headed towards the platform. The pain I mentioned earlier began to fade as I got farther away from the hospital, and when I finally arrived home, it disappeared completely. After packing my bag with running clothes, we all went to sleep because the next day, after waking up at four o'clock, we would embark on another two-hour car journey. I was excited because I had been preparing for these races for a long time. It was my debut in the Spartan Race. I had a rough idea of what to expect from watching various videos online. I was also looking forward to meeting friends from the club. I hoped that for a moment, I could forget about the reality surrounding me.

Even such high obstacles didn't stop us from completing the race

The alarm went off exactly at four in the morning, and I barely dragged myself out of bed. Fatigue was hard to ignore, and that morning, instead of savoring my favorite brewed coffee, I drank an energy drink and took another one for the road. We packed our bags into the car and set off on our journey.

As I was driving, I couldn't stop thinking about our daughter. Along the way, we took a brief detour from the highway so that Eve and Sebastian could have breakfast while I settled for an energy bar. Heavy meals were out of the question since I had over thirteen kilometers of running ahead of me. We continued on our way, and Sebastian was eager to get out of the car even before I had a chance to park. When he saw where we had arrived, he was very excited, but he started crying when I told him that it would be me running, not him. He was deeply disappointed, but the minimum age for Spartan Race was four years old. I went to register and meet up with my friends. We all had our start in the same wave, around 10 a.m. From the pre-race stories, we had a rough idea of what to expect on the course. It was said to have plenty of hills. Before starting my warm-up, I positioned myself near the starting line and observed the Elite wave of runners beginning their race.

Father and son, after crossing the finish line

Always observing those better than myself, I gain greater inspiration. Once the wave of men and women started, I returned to the spot where everyone from my wave was gathered. The clock was nearing ten o'clock, and my mind was focused on one goal, to finish the race. We all entered the field in front of the starting line, loud music blaring from the speakers, and at the signal, we all set off. I ran about five kilometers, and then questions about Natalie started to occupy my mind. I had a faint hope that being at such a sporting event would allow me to momentarily forget about everything. But it was impossible. No matter how hard I tried, I couldn't forget. I completed the race in just under three hours. It wasn't an outstanding result for me, but I had never run on such a hilly course before, and the satisfaction of finishing was still very motivating for me. I bid farewell to everyone and headed back home. The next day, I had another race in the same location, but at a shorter distance. On the way, we got a bit hungry, so we took an exit from the highway to grab a quick bite. In the meantime, my wife called the hospital to inquire about Natalie's condition. We didn't expect anything alarming. The doctors reassured us once again that everything was progressing well. The swelling on her head was decreasing, the wound was healing, and the irritated knee was being treated with oint-ment. We returned home calmly, and I quickly took a hot bath to pre-vent muscle soreness.

The next day, we woke up at the same time as on Saturday and set off on the same route as usual, making a stop at the same service sta-tion. However, the hot bath didn't help me much. Each time, my body was heavily affected by the races, and every time I got in or out of the car, I had to hold onto something. The hot bath from the previous day didn't provide much relief.

Before the next obstacle

We arrived at the location, and once again I had the pleasure of me-eting some of my friends whom I had seen the previous day. As I pre-pared for the warm-up, I knew that despite the shorter distance, this race would be more challenging. Fortunately, despite limited mobility in my limbs, I managed to complete it. Afterward, I sat on the grass for about ten minutes, lacking the strength to stand up. I was incredibly exhausted. Running two races in one weekend was something new for me, but it was time to return to everyday life. Before heading home, Eve called the hospital. She heard exactly the same update as the pre-vious day. When I returned home and everyone had gone to sleep, I hung my hard-earned medals on the wall. One with blue accents and the other with red.

Pleasant Surprise

As cheesy as it sounds, maybe the good days will make it worth getting through the bad ones.

Jasmine Warga

On Monday, July 15th, at seven in the morning, the alarm clock rang. At first, I didn't know what was happening. I was abruptly awakened from sleep, but after a moment, I realized that it was simply another day. When I tried to get out of bed to turn off the alarm, my body refused to cooperate. I had never experienced such intense muscle soreness before. Eventually, I managed to perform the planned task, luckily without waking anyone up, and went downstairs to make my favorite brewed coffee. Descending the stairs, I had to hold onto the railing and take one step at a time. It looked quite comical, but it meant that I had quite a workout over the weekend. As I moved from the living room to the kitchen, the first thing I did was glance at the medals hanging on the wall. I smiled widely. While sipping my coffee, I prepared fried eggs with bacon and chives for everyone. Breakfast had to be hearty because once again we would be spending the entire day away from home.

When I barely got into the car to drive to the train station, I knew that the journey from the platform to the hospital would take us a bit longer than usual. I took small steps, and the biggest challenge was crossing the bridge over the busy road just before the hospital. Fortunately, there was an elevator in the building; I didn't even want to think about taking the stairs. As we entered the ward, we immediately noticed that our daughter wasn't in the crib where she had been lying before. But before we could ask where she was, the doctors showed us a room behind closed doors where they had moved our child. A lady who happened to be taking care of Natalie that day entered the room with us. She explained that the reason for her relocation was the quarantine in the hospital, and other children from the ward had also been placed in similar rooms to avoid the risk of infection. After providing us with this information, she said she had to step out for about fifteen minutes, but she would come back to us afterward. Natalie was asleep. She was lying on her side, and we were happy to see her again. We had only been apart for two days, but we missed her terribly. Sebastian approached to greet his sister, slipping his little hand through the rails. Natalie tightly grasped his finger and didn't want to let go. Siblings together always made a beautiful sight, and this time was no exception. Eve sat down to breastfeed, and I took out my phone to capture a few photos as a memento.

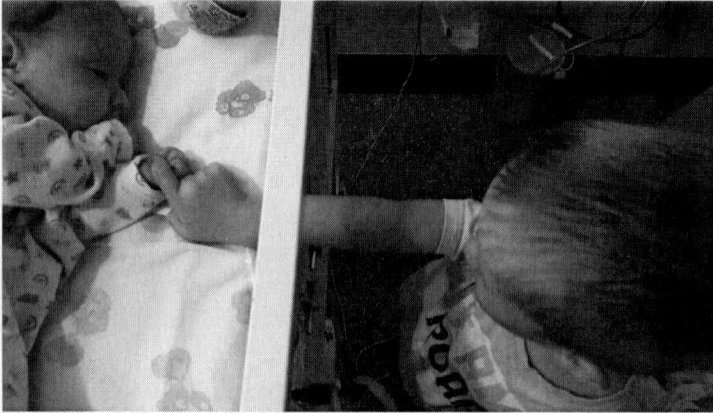

Brother with sister

When our son started whining, we once again put on cartoons for him. He took advantage of it, watching those cartoons that we usually didn't allow him to watch at home. We didn't have time to check his phone every five minutes to see what he was watching. Initially, we were in control of it, but over time, we stopped. We looked at Natalie and wondered when they would disconnect her catheter. I didn't quite understand why they even connected it in the first place. We were so tired that we let go of that question for the day. We just wanted to sit down and spend as much time as possible with her. We visited her every day, and each time we could see an improvement. The wound on her back was healing nicely, and the knee was no longer red, but a small mark remained. We lost track of time and couldn't fully comprehend how long it had all been going on. Sometimes we had to think about what day of the week it was. Sebastian's summer vacation was coming to an end, and we really wanted Natalie to be discharged before that time. One day, during our regular visit, the doctor approached us and delivered good news. The plastic surgeon discharged the child from his care, stating that the wound had healed and there was no need for further observation. Another good piece of information conveyed by the doctor was that the catheter had been removed, and now they would focus on weighing diapers to check if they were heavy. However, the most important news was that they intended to discharge her home within two weeks, and if all went well, it could be within one week. We were overjoyed. We had been waiting for such news for a long time. Finally, our daughter would be with us, and those burdensome trips to the hospital would come to an end. After returning home, we informed our immediate family about the situation. Everyone was happy that it was finally over, and everything would return to normal.

Sitting in the evening with a glass of wine, we eagerly awaited the arrival of the next day when we would go to see our Natalie. We raised a toast to the good news while watching one of our favorite TV series.

The beginning of the next day, despite the routine of the past weeks, was completely different from the previous ones. Smiles never left our faces, and our moods were so uplifted that we felt like we were floating. We were so joyful that before heading to the hospital, we stopped to have our favorite Thai dish and then went to the shopping mall for a little shopping. Everything started falling into place, and we were eager to bring her home that very day.

We already knew the way to the hospital by heart, and whenever the weather was favorable, we would choose to take a walk. That time, the clear sky and heat accompanied us throughout the day. Once we were in the hospital, we had a chance to cool down a bit, but only in the main corridor. When we entered the ward, we felt warmth again, but fortunately not as intense as outside. We went straight to Natalie and waited for the doctor who was taking care of her that day. Our eyes fell upon a large, white piece of paper attached to the front of her crib. It contained all the information about her condition and her progress. We were particularly interested in whether her head was getting smaller and how heavy the wet diapers were. The entry mentioned that her head was progressing as expected, but there was no information about the diapers. So we had to wait for the update, hoping it would be positive. After about fifteen minutes, the attending nurse came and informed us that the diapers were heavy. It was a very good sign. It meant that the child was emptying her bladder, and in cases of spina bifida in the lumbar-sacral region, it is common for something to accumulate, requiring catheterization. It was truly a pleasant surprise.

After a while, a nurse in a different-colored apron entered the room. It was purple, unlike the aprons worn by the other nurses. We had no idea why. No one had informed us about such a visit, so we were unsure of what to expect. The unfamiliar nurse introduced herself as a specialist in urinary tract issues and came to teach us how to catheterize Natalie. We weren't particularly thrilled with this information. Compared to what our daughter had already been through, it seemed like a minor issue, but still another unpleasant matter. On that day, she only provided us with the theory and demonstrated the process once. She took out a tube from her bag, and upon opening it, a moist, rubbery, small stick emerged. It was a type of catheter that we were supposed to use. She also explained how many times a day we should do it, depending on the amount of urine that would come out. If none, once a day; if over ten milliliters, twice a day; if over twenty, three times a day, and so on. She bid us farewell, asking if we would be in the hospital in three days. She promised to explain everything again in more detail at that time. We confirmed our presence and then returned to enjoy the rest of the day.

Unexpected Turn of Events

I learned that courage was not the absence of fear, but the triumph over it. C e brave man is not he who does not feel afraid, but he who conquers that fear.

Nelson Mandela

A week has passed since we were informed about the possibility of an early discharge of our child from the hospital. However, after a week, it hasn't happened yet, possibly due to the training we had on catheterization. On that day, when we arrived to see Natalie, we asked the doctors how much longer it would take. Our weekly train tickets were running out, and we secretly hoped that we wouldn't have to buy more because the prices for the South Elmsall to Leeds route were exorbitant. Not only did the railway charge a lot for the tickets but there wasn't a week without train delays or cancellations. Unfortunately, on the way back, we had to purchase another set of weekly tickets because the doctors wanted to make sure that we would be able to handle her at home. Moreover, it turned out that she was still being examined by neurologists. It greatly frustrated us at that time. First, they would say one thing, and then it would turn out to be completely different, and the nurses informed us that it was not up to them to decide the patient's discharge, but to the doctors. Once again, we spent several hours at the hospital. The daily commutes put a strain on our budget, and eventually, we had to tighten our expenses. Additionally, every day we would come home exhausted, with no time or energy to play with Sebastian, and it was evident that he needed it. We tried to compensate him by buying some toy cars or Lego sets from time to time. However, we were aware that this temporary solution was heading in the wrong direction because no toys could replace a parent for a child.

For the following days, nothing changed. Each day looked the same, but only until one day when we arrived to see Natalie, and my wife noticed that the baby was making a faint wheezing sound while sleeping. She asked the nurse to call the doctor because she wanted to discuss it. She became quite worried about it, but when the doctor arrived, he said that an examination was not necessary. He explained to us that some infants have that characteristic wheezing sound, and it usually subsides on its own after some time. We acknowledged this information, but knowing my wife and her nature, I knew that she would keep thinking about it. I didn't blame her for it; I always tried to understand her. Besides, I always tried to support and comfort her whenever there was a reason to do so. Whenever a worrying situation arose, not necessarily related to the child, it would play out similarly. During the entire journey back home, during dinner, and before bed, I listened to her repeating the same concerns—how she didn't like Natalie's breathing sound and how it worried her. I tried to explain to her that we are not experts and that she should listen to what the doctor said. Apparently, Natalie needed a bit more time. Nothing helped. Once again, my arguments were pushed aside. I decided it wasn't worth my nerves, so I resolved not to bring up the topic again and simply wait for the time the doctor mentioned. The next morning was no different from the previous ones, except for the expression on my wife's face. I didn't bring up yesterday's issue; I just wanted to be at the hospital with Natalie as soon as possible. Yes, we arrived quite early because we took an earlier train, but my joy disappeared from my face when my wife's concerns were confirmed. The child was connected to oxygen. The strange wheezing sound became more intense, and Natalie was struggling to breathe. Things took a turn for the worse. Complications arose that were not supposed to happen. The nurses who had been taking care of Natalie in the past 24 hours informed us that she was now under the observation of doctors from a different department. The staff attached three more colorful cables to measure various bodily functions. It was terribly cumbersome; every time I wanted to hold the baby, I had to be careful not to disconnect any of them. A few times, accidentally, I bumped into one of the cables, and it simply detached, triggering a loud alarm on the monitor.

Natalie remained under the observation of doctors for about a week. Her breathing significantly improved, so they decided to disconnect the additional oxygen. The baby was able to breathe on her own, although the sound resembling a rooster's crowing did not disappear. Additional tests and X-rays of the chest and neck were ordered. Fortunately, in her case, we didn't have to wait long. Everyone was aware of how serious the situation was. The results were conclusive. Additional growth was found in her throat that needed to be removed. After this procedure, the child's breathing and voice should return to normal. We were shocked when we heard the diagnosis. Natalie was to undergo her third surgery, although they said it would be a procedure under general anesthesia. We signed the papers, giving our consent to the surgery. We were also informed that nasal tubes would be inserted for feeding purposes, as Natalie would not be able to eat for some time after the operation. Eve was asked to continue expressing milk into bottles and leave them at the hospital. The most important thing was that the mother's milk was continuously supplied to the tiny body. The surgery was scheduled for two days after the problem was detected. I could see that my wife was devastated. I tried to comfort her, assuring her that everything would be fine after this and that we would bring Natalie home soon. But it was in vain. Once again, none of my arguments reached her.

The day of the surgery arrived. Natalie was taken early in the morning, and they couldn't determine the exact time she would be brought back to the ward. Everything took several hours. In the afternoon, they brought the child back with the news that the procedure was successful. In the meantime, our daughter had been awakened and was slowly recovering. I felt relieved when I heard those words. We decided to let her rest and come back the next day. We were exhausted, and we didn't think about anything else except getting some sleep. Our son was with us every day, and his fatigue was also becoming apparent. He didn't understand what was happening to his sister, and he often just got bored. Whenever we had a spare moment, we tried to play or talk with him, but during that time, we had very little energy for such things. The situation was so chaotic that managing time for Sebastian overwhelmed us, and he significantly suffered from all of it.

The next morning, we arrived at the hospital early with the hope that everything would be fine with our little one. Unfortunately, the strange wheezing sound didn't go away, and we noticed the oxygen equipment near her again. We had no idea what had happened and why the child needed oxygen again. Why hadn't the strange wheezing sound disappeared? This time, the doctors were unable to answer our questions because they themselves didn't know what was happening. We thought that after the procedure, everything would return to normal, but it turned out that the growth in her throat was not the cause of the strange breathing sound. So we asked if the procedure was necessary. In response, we were told that it was necessary because that part was somewhat obstructing and the additional tissue had to be removed. Whatever happened, it didn't go away. We had to focus on Natalie because her condition had drastically changed. We could see that her chest was sinking deeply when she was restless. We had never seen such a phenomenon before. One test after another followed. Head and throat ultrasounds and others. The race against time had begun.

Intensive Care

We cannot change the direction of the wind, but we can adjust our sails.

Andreas Pflüger

While holding my little girl in my arms, I looked deeply into her eyes. Tears welled up as I witnessed the suffering of my tiny daughter. I felt helpless as salty droplets fell onto Natalie. A few colorful cables were connected to her tiny body, along with two feeding tubes inserted into her nose and oxygen. The abundance of these devices sometimes made it difficult to hold her. The cables tangled, and the oxygen tube would occasionally slip out of her tiny nostrils despite the adhesive strips holding it in place. Whenever Natalie breathed, there was a constant strange sound. When she became agitated, her voice became strained, and her oxygen saturation dropped, resulting in an increased need for oxygen supply. A massive patient chart lay in front of the crib, where new data was constantly being recorded. Based on this information, every specialist doctor entering the room could determine whether the child's condition had improved, worsened, or remained unchanged. In the case of our daughter, it deteriorated day by day.

I dealt with stress naturally, fortunately, my mental strength was strong enough that I didn't have to take any calming medication. A cup of herbal tea with lemon balm was enough, and it made me feel much better. My wife also avoided taking any medication, but it was evident that she was struggling more with the situation. Every day we prayed to God for her health. We believed that faith can work miracles, and in this matter, we couldn't afford to lose hope. God had shown His power before. We listened to interviews and stories of people whose children suddenly recovered without any scientific explanation. Our faith allowed us to keep going, even though life threw obstacles at us every day. The child's condition was worsening, the oxygen level was increased, and the doctors were still searching for a way to help her.

One day, as I was sitting on a red bench, some parts of its paint peeling off, waiting for the train, my phone rang. It turned out that the child's condition had deteriorated to such an extent that the doctors decided to transfer her to the intensive care unit. It was another blow straight to the heart, but we were determined to keep fighting. When we arrived at the hospital, they quickly directed us to the room where they had moved our child. We had no idea what to expect. This time, we saw more monitors, and cables, and, unfortunately, every crib was occupied. Seeing the sad eyes of the parents from the previous room made me feel terrible. However, what I experienced in Natalie's new room completely overwhelmed me. Most of the parents were constantly crying while holding their little ones or leaning over their cribs. It was a true nightmare. We found ourselves in a place that resembled hell on earth. The doctors pointed us to a crib for our little one, additional monitors, and even more cables connected to her tiny body.

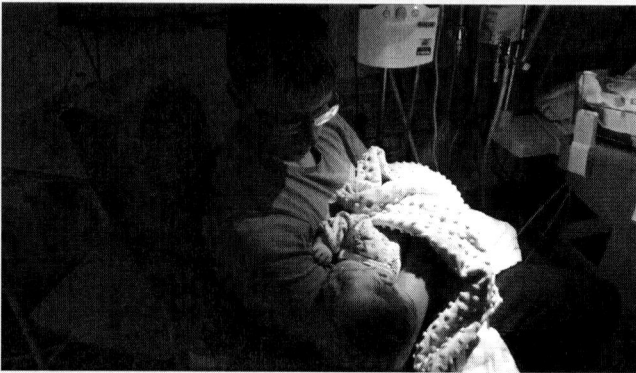

A photo from the intensive care unit taken on the first day after Natalie was transferred from the postoperative ward

The heavy breathing of our little one knocked us off our feet. After consulting with the doctors, we learned that another head ultrasound for the child would be performed tomorrow. The examination had to be done under general anesthesia to ensure the most accurate results.

Initially, we thought about staying in the hospital for that one day, but it quickly dawned on us that it wouldn't be a good idea due to Sebastian. After two hours of a nightmare, we made our way home, sweaty and exhausted.

We were already so worn out by everything that on August 17th, my mother flew in to help us a bit with Sebastian. Straight from Leeds Bradford Airport, we went to the hospital to visit our daughter, and then we stopped by the amusement park that had been set up in the center a few days earlier. Our son went on rides with his grandmother, while my wife and I sat down on a bench to catch our breath. Less than an hour passed, and we still had one more stop planned. An enormous ice cream sundae was served right in the heart of the park. Granted, we had to pay a bit for it, but it was truly worth it. That dose of sweetness lifted all of our moods, but I felt as if I had just put on a mask with a smile painted on it, hiding the sadness beneath. When I closed my eyes for a moment to rest after the sweet dessert, my imagination kept showing me the machines connected to Natalie. And the numbers constantly changing on the screens. I tried not to think about it, but I didn't see how I could avoid it.

My mother's visit lasted only a few days. However, it was enough. Everyone managed to take a break from the daily routine, and finally, our child was also smiling. We devoted our time to him, and having my mother's help made it easier for us. As we said goodbye to her at the bus stop, we heard her reassuring us not to worry, that everything would be fine, we just needed to believe deeply in it. Positive thinking attracts positive energy and has a great impact on us and our surroundings. It wasn't an easy task, but I tried to think positively.

Another day arrived, and Eve asked me what time I wanted to go to our daughter. I replied that I would go after I finish my run. I couldn't forget about sports either. In October, I had a trail half marathon with obstacles coming up, which was quite a challenge for me since I had never run such a distance before, let alone with additional obstacles. Besides, engaging in sports allowed me to think clearly. It's not without reason that they say sports are beneficial to health. Both physical and mental well-being helped me maintain emotional balance. After completing my training, we went to the hospital. When the ultrasound examination was over, Natalie was once again connected to the oxygen machine. We asked how long we would have to wait for the results, and we were told it would take one day. We had no choice but to wait. We hoped that the doctors would find the cause of our child's sudden deterioration and be able to implement appropriate treatment.

The next day, we requested the prompt delivery of the ultrasound results, but we had to wait a little longer for the neurologist. While waiting for the specialist, we stayed with our little one surrounded by a tangle of colored cables. Honestly, I don't know how much time passed before the neurologist appeared, but it was certainly more than just an hour. The senior doctor informed us that Natalie had a type of inflammation at the back of her head, which could be pressing on the nerves responsible for proper breathing. To make matters worse, there was no specific medication for it, and the inflammation had to resolve on its own. He also recommended another ultrasound, this time of the throat, to find the cause of the strange wheezing during breathing. The condition of our little one continued to deteriorate, and the doctors had no good news for us. We had to somehow get through it, holding onto a deep belief that a miracle from God would happen, and our child would recover. Despite constantly falling from exhaustion and being bombarded with negative information, our faith kept us going. Days went by, but the inflammation didn't improve. Holding our little one, I observed other families in the same room. They were despairing, and some seemed to have lost the strength to continue fighting their own battles of the mind.

We returned home and connected with Eve's mother via video call to tell her what had been happening. During the conversation, the phone unexpectedly rang, and Eve had to answer it. It turned out to be a call from the hospital, informing us that Natalie had been placed on a ventilator due to a sudden and severe deterioration of her condition. We reconnected with our family and relayed the latest information. Our plan had been to watch a movie with my wife and have a glass of wine, but instead, we went to bed with teary eyes.

I didn't sleep well that night. I barely slept for three hours, constantly imagining how it would look. I had never seen a child connected to a ventilator before, and I couldn't even imagine it. Yes, I could have searched the internet and looked it up, but I didn't want to do that.

As I crossed the threshold of the room where our child was, I saw about seven doctors wearing different colored lab coats, doing something by Natalie's bedside. One person was writing something on a huge chart, another was pressing various buttons on a machine, and the rest were consulting with each other. They all greeted us, forcing artificial smiles on their faces, and then went their separate ways. Except for one tall, dark-skinned man with glasses and a "consultant" badge. He presented the situation to us and explained why our daughter had been put on a ventilator. The readings from the machines connected to Natalie the previous day were very concerning, so the doctors felt compelled to take this action. They were also obligated to make a phone call if the parents were not present at the hospital at that moment to inform them about the whole situation.

We were able to understand the procedure, but what we couldn't comprehend was why everything had deteriorated within twenty-four hours. So we asked the consultant about their plans for the next steps. The response was quick: they intended to keep her under the machine for a few more days, then disconnect the ventilator and observe how the child would respond. In the meantime, they informed us that a consultation would be organized, which was necessary in such cases.

The days passed, and Natalie's condition showed no signs of improvement. The ventilator was essential for her. Every time the doctors attempted to remove the device from her mouth, the child was unable to breathe independently. Her chest would sink deeply when disconnected from the machines, clearly indicating that the little girl was struggling. There was never a day when there was an available spot in the intensive care unit. Out of the corner of my eye, I even noticed a family adorning their child's bed with pictures taken at the hospital, implying that they had been there for quite some time. It all overwhelmed me more and more. I constantly saw doctors rushing from one bed to another. Sometimes, within five minutes, they would whisk away children for urgent surgeries. Not all of them returned.

If someone were to ask me if I have ever been to hell, I can confidently answer, yes. Such a place could definitely be compared to it.

There was no indication that our little daughter would leave that ward. All we could do was pray for her and for all the children in that dreadful room.

Impromptu Baptism

It will be beautiful, despite everything. Just put on comfortable shoes because you have a whole life ahead of you.

Pope John Paul II

The sun had set, leaving behind a beautiful sky adorned with soothing colors, and we talked with our loved ones during that time. Our child was in a tragic state. No one knew what to expect and how it would all end. It never crossed our minds that such a situation could arise, where our little one might not make it and would depart to the Kingdom of Heaven. We listened to various lectures by priests, but only one, authored by the late Father Kaczkowski, showed us that we cannot control everything. He advised us that in hopeless situations, we should simply let the person go, whether it be a child, a teenager, or an elderly person. He also spoke about how families keep individuals alive at any cost, unaware of their suffering. Despite that lecture, we still didn't allow the thought that we could also face a similar situation to enter our minds.

The climactic moment arrived, and my wife and I couldn't hold back our tears. She sat crying at the kitchen table, while I hunched over the counter between the stove and the refrigerator. I held my head in my hands, unable to gather my own thoughts. In the background, the song "The Sound of Silence" played quite loudly, effectively drawing even more tears from me. In a state of complete exhaustion, we went to sleep, but I must admit that letting ourselves cry allowed us to breathe a sigh of relief. We had literally expelled all the emotions that had been accumulating like a snowball.

Another day passed just like the previous ones, with the only difference being that we couldn't take our little one out of the crib due to the constantly running machine. We could only stand by her bedside, pray, and nothing more. Soon, we had our first consultation ahead of us.

As we looked at our little one's suffering, we realized that we had completely forgotten about a very important matter. That's when we made the decision together to baptize Natalie in the hospital. We, as parents, as the priest might not be able to reach the hospital in time. At first, we were unsure if it was possible, but considering the situation and the green light from the doctors, we decided to proceed. Even during that simple ceremony, we felt that we were doing everything as it should be. We were instructed on how to perform the ritual. We were to pour a little tap water into a tiny vessel, stand by the baby's side, and recite a prayer while gently sprinkling her with water. We were also to add that we were doing this as parents and that God would hear our prayer. At first, I didn't know how to approach it. There were so many people around, and we were supposed to stand over the child and recite a prayer with tap water. We entered the room, played cartoons on Sebastian's phone, and without hesitation, Eve asked for a plastic cup and went to get water. She asked the doctors not to disturb us for a while because we needed to pray. They listened to our request and moved away from the bed. The prayer had to come straight from the heart. I stood on one side of the crib, and Eve stood on the other. We recited the prayer out loud while gently sprinkling Natalie's head with water. We didn't care if anyone was watching us at that moment. In addition to water, our tears also fell on the child. Tears of love, because there was no other way to describe them. Salty drops fell one after another, and despite her critical condition, the child looked into my eyes and her mother's eyes throughout the ceremony. I felt the power of the prayer we had just performed. I told my daughter that I had said good-bye to her twice already, and I wouldn't do it a third time. She must live, and the inflammation in the back of her head must disappear! I said, "Satan, leave my daughter's body! Go away and never return! Get out! We don't want you here!"

We felt relieved in our hearts. If the worst scenario were to happen back then, and our child didn't survive, we knew she would be in the hands of God. As soon as I snapped out of the trance and began looking around the room, all the families around us started averting their gaze. Perhaps they didn't understand the power of faith and blamed

God for their child being in the hospital. It wasn't our place to judge. We wanted to focus on our children, and I knew we had done a good job.

The child remained intubated for a whole week. A dark-skinned consultant informed us that they would attempt to remove the tube and see how the child would cope. However, he also warned us that there was a possibility they might need to use the respirator again. We watched as the entire operation to remove the tube from the little mouth unfolded. The doctors disconnected the respirator while increasing the oxygen to a fairly high level. Little Natalie looked into my eyes and started crying. It appeared that way because the child was unable to produce any sound. At first, I became worried that something was wrong. I asked the nurse to have the person in the tie come back here because I had a few questions. Initially, I asked why the child wasn't speaking. The response I received was that it was normal after intubation and would take a few days before she starts making sounds again. I was reassured. We had nothing else to do but rejoice in the fact that the little girl was in better condition and breathing without the respirator. Disconnecting the machine allowed for a throat ultrasound to be performed to investigate why the strange voice hadn't disappeared. The child's condition had improved only slightly, but the decision was made to keep her in intensive care.

Several days passed, and then our daughter was taken downstairs for a scheduled ultrasound. They had to perform it again under general anesthesia to obtain more accurate results. This time, knowing how medical procedures go, we didn't inquire about getting the results as quickly as possible. We knew we would have to wait at least a day. However, this time, two whole days passed before we were informed of the results. Just when everything seemed to be falling apart, we received more bad news. We learned that the inflammation at the back of her head could be pressing on the nerves responsible for the vocal cords, which had stopped functioning. They should be opening and closing, but in Natalie's case, they were found to be constantly open. Another blow straight to the heart. We started wondering if this was some kind of test for us if we would be able to endure all this pain and go through it together. Obstacles were constantly being thrown in our path. The first consultation was scheduled for two days later. My wife cried constantly and said that there was an eighty percent chance they would suggest a tracheotomy. Once again, I tried to calm Eve down and explained to her that she had read nonsense on the internet. I refused to accept that doctors might propose such a solution. The last two days were very difficult, and while sitting at the computer late into the night, I tried to find as much valuable information as possible.

Consultation

Keep all uncertainty hidden beneath the surface. On the outside, you must appear as solid as a stone.

Melinda Salisbury

Passing by the oncology ward, I noticed a hairless boy in a wheelchair. I saw him watching me with his eyes. After that experience, I began to ponder which was worse: the intensive therapy where our child lies or the oncology ward? Perhaps both were equally challenging? One thing was certain, both rooms were like hell, lacking only demons brandishing pitchforks. The consultation was scheduled for two o'clock, but I'm not sure. Anyway, the timing of the conversation was the least important. What mattered was who would be there and how it would unfold. First, we visited our daughter, wiping her with a damp cloth, changing her diaper, and cuddling her. Holding the little one in our arms, we witnessed a human tragedy. A tearful family rushed out of the room separated by doors in the intensive therapy area, followed by doctors with stone-faced expressions. It turned out that one of the children couldn't make it. All the machines, even more than Natalie had, were disconnected, and through a small window in the door, one could see a weeping nurse holding a lifeless baby wrapped in a blanket. That sight will stay with me for the rest of my life. After a moment, the consultant arrived and informed us where to go. Due to that distressing experience, I momentarily forgot about our scheduled consultation. We entered the corridor behind the reception. Across from us were locked, brown doors, and behind them was the designated room where almost everyone had already gathered. One doctor was missing, and his lateness was due to his duties. We entered the room, and the first thing we heard from the consultant among the gathered individuals was whether we would like some coffee or tea. Biscuits were also placed on the table, sprinkled with sugar, and everything looked as if we had just visited friends we hadn't seen in a long time. However, it was only an illusion created in my mind. After a while, everyone introduced themselves and asked if the translator should tell us everything or just the parts we wouldn't understand. We chose the latter option due to our good command of the English language. We requested a translator because of the difficult, specialized medical language, some aspects of which might be challenging for us to grasp. We sat on the couch, and on our right side sat a blonde woman with shoulder-length hair. She started by asking if we knew the purpose of our gathering here. We replied that we did. They presented us with the entire history of our daughter, which was described in a familiar gray folder with a blue elastic band. Hospital procedures required it every time. The next stage of the meeting was the delivery of prognoses and information about the planned steps toward Natalka's full recovery. They told us that the little girl couldn't breathe without additional oxygen and proposed another surgery. Tracheotomy was the best solution for them. For them and for the child, as it would alleviate her suffering. Before I could say anything, I looked at my wife, her tears streaming down her face, as she foresaw the worst-case scenario. To the doctors' surprise, we refused the operation and asked them to find another solution, and above all, to give the child more time. We deeply believed that the inflammation would disappear spontaneously, and that prayer was all that was needed. We didn't mention this to the doctors because we didn't know their beliefs, and our arguments might not have resonated with them in any way.

The consultation concluded by noting everything that was said during it. We returned to the room and spent some more time with our daughter. We spoke to her, telling her to be strong and not to give up.

We didn't know what to make of it all. We desperately wanted our daughter to be with us, but on the other hand, subjecting her to another surgery with such serious consequences was out of the question. The little one fell asleep in my wife's arms, and after placing her in the crib, we headed towards the exit, already knowing the way by heart. As we left the hospital, we passed the homeless man with a long beard once again, along with his dog sitting on a piece of carpet with a red cup in front of him, presumably for coffee.

After returning home, there was nothing left for us to do but inform the family, have a cup of melissa tea, and go to sleep. Sebastian fell asleep in his car seat and didn't even wake up when I transferred him to his crib. Tomorrow, we were facing another physically and mentally demanding day, albeit sunny, but the weather interested us the least.

Time

Love is the supreme force of the universe; it is what sets the stars in motion.

Dante Alighieri

Days passed, and Natalie's condition slightly improved. Within a week, we had additional consultations aimed at psychologically preparing us to agree to the tracheotomy. Of course, we persistently stood by our decision, which the doctors were not pleased with. In the meantime, during my silent recitation of the Lord's Prayer over Natalie, a consultant approached. This time, a different one, whose facial features made him look like he came from India. What he conveyed, interrupting my prayer, caught me off guard. He straightforwardly asked if we would agree to a minor gastrostomy procedure because the girl had reflux, and the procedure would facilitate her feeding. My wife and I looked at him in disbelief, wondering how he could speak about such matters with such calmness. Most likely, he had already performed hundreds of such operations or had similar conversations, and it didn't faze him in the least. We responded that there was absolutely nothing to discuss. The man, with slightly wavy black hair, simply acknowledged that he understood and left the room. As if it weren't enough, new complications kept arising constantly. I was surprised by how we managed to endure all of this mentally without taking any calming pills.

When we arrived at the hospital the next day and entered the intensive care unit, we immediately noticed that Natalie's crib was empty. The first thought that crossed our minds was that she might have been taken for further tests, of which there were plenty scheduled ahead. However, upon checking the calendar, we discovered that Natalie had no tests scheduled for that day. A nurse quickly approached us and informed us that the child's condition had improved enough for the doctors to decide that she could return to the previous room where she had been staying. Upon hearing these words, I saw a smile appear on my wife's face, a smile that I hadn't seen in several long weeks. A glimmer of hope emerged that maybe our little one could get through this, and eventually, we would bring her home. Knowing exactly where the previous room was, we immediately headed in that direction. The only difference was that this time the baby was lying in a crib on the right side, just after passing through the main, brown doors with tiny built-in windows. Everything was familiar to us. The child was still on high oxygen, and feeding tubes were still in her nostrils. The peculiar sound hadn't disappeared; every time she breathed, her chest sank deeply, and when Natalie became agitated, there was an immediate need to increase the oxygen temporarily. I started discussing with my wife how prayer was helping, not only our own prayers but also those of our family and friends. Many people were praying for Natalie's health, which kept our spirits up. We also knew that Natalie could sense our presence. Every time we came to the hospital, and she heard our voices (if she wasn't asleep at that moment), her eyes would widen, and she would start looking around to figure out where the voices were coming from.

One afternoon, a colleague from work called me and asked if he could come to the hospital with his family to visit Natalie. Without hesitation, we agreed to the visit, mentioning that there was a virus on the ward and only mothers were allowed in. We also mentioned that we would try to talk to the doctors, but we couldn't promise that they would be able to see the baby. The next day, our friend and his family arrived at the hospital, and we went out to greet them. This was a person who did something extraordinary for us. He prepared a presentation about Natalie, which he showed in the church on a large screen in front of a crowd of people. We had no idea about it beforehand, and he didn't give away his idea, only asking for a photo of our daughter. Everything was recorded so that we could watch it later. Tears filled my eyes as I saw how many strangers were praying for our daughter's health. Besides the introduction, which was in English, the entire film was in Portuguese. These people prayed aloud and fervently, and it meant so much to us. Looking at the screen of the phone from which the recording was played, we recited the Lord's Prayer.

After greeting our friends, we went to the café located inside the hospital building. Sebastian and their daughter, who was around the same age, were running around the room, occasionally stopping by the ice cream fridge and looking at the colorful wrappers inside. We had a great time talking, but the café's closing hours were approaching. So we finished our drinks and headed outside the hospital. There were comfortable benches around trees, where we sat down. The beautiful weather allowed us to enjoy the outdoors. We mainly talked about our faith and how we believed that God would heal our daughter and bring her out of the situation she was in. As it was getting close to 7 PM, we said goodbye to our guests and went back to Natalie for the last half an hour of the day to spend some time with her.

Sitting at home in the evening, we felt more at ease. We were glad that our daughter was getting slightly better. Almost every evening, we would talk to our family and tell them about what had happened during the day. And this time was no exception. After about ten minutes of conversation, the suggestion came up to persuade the doctors if we could take our little girl outside. Since birth, she had never been outside the hospital walls, and so much time had passed. Fresh air should help her. That was the least we could do. There was nothing left for us but to go early in the morning and present our request. Entering the ward, we asked the nurse on duty, who was taking care of Natalie that day, if we could take her outside with the assistance of a doctor. At first, she said it might be inconvenient because it was Friday and there weren't many doctors in the hospital. If any of them had a moment, they would try to arrange an outing. Luckily, we didn't have to wait long, and after about an hour, they informed us that the doctor was on the way, and soon we would be able to go outside. A baby stroller, which was part of the hospital's equipment, was brought to the ward. The necessary monitoring machine, keeping track of all the numbers, was placed in the free space in the stroller, right next to the baby's feet. At first, we thought we would take Natalie outside the hospital to the place where we had sat during the visit with our friends. However, that was not possible. We could only go to the terrace near the top of the building with the baby. There was a fairly large terrace with benches surrounded by colorful flowers. We were happy that our child would be able to breathe some fresh air for the first time. To look at the lush vegetation and listen to the birds singing, occasionally perching on the railing. We went out for literally five minutes when unexpectedly a security guard came and politely asked everyone to leave the area. The reason for locking the doors separating the stuffy corridor from the place with bronze benches was that a helicopter would be landing one floor above, and hospital procedures required the terrace one floor below to be closed during that time. So we had to find another solution. The assisting doctor told us that we could go outside but on the other side of the hospital entrance. So we took the elevator down and went towards the exit. This time, instead of fresh air, the smell, or rather a stench, of burnt cigarettes hit my nostrils. People in hospital gowns, some holding drip stands, were huddled outside the building with a cigarette in hand. I could never understand how strong that addiction could be, since I've never smoked myself. Apparently, being hooked up to an IV drip and visiting the hospital weren't enough to quit the habit. We walked a bit further to avoid the smell of cigarettes. We sat on a bench, and then Eve took the baby out of the stroller and held her in her arms. Natalie saw green leaves on the tree growing nearby for the first time. She started looking around, discovering new shapes and forms. The assisting doctor in a dark blue gown asked if we would like to take a group photo. Without hesitation, we handed her the phone, and she captured one of the most wonderful memories for us. We sat there for a while, trying to calm ourselves. All the negative thoughts vanished, and we were simply enjoying the moment. We felt great and didn't want to go back to the ward, but feeding time was approaching, and it was necessary. As soon as we returned to the hospital, the baby fell asleep. We told the nurse that we wouldn't be there this weekend and asked if they could change Natalie's position more frequently because her knee hadn't healed yet. There was a small mark indicating the beginning of a pressure sore, although tiny, it was still visible.

Wandering through the outlet, we explored all the shops, and then we went to the arcade to somehow compensate Sebastian for the daily trips to the hospital. Unfortunately, apart from a short stay in Poland before Natalie's birth, our son hadn't had a vacation at all. On Saturday,

right after my run, which always started at nine in the morning and covered a distance of five kilometers, we headed to Castleford for some
small shopping.

The first outing of Natalie outside the hospital walls documented by our assisting doctor

We also had plans to go to the cinema, but we weren't sure if our three-
year-old would sit through the whole movie. We decided to give up on
that idea and instead opted for the attractions set up outside the building where the cinema was located. There were restaurants, a ski lift,
sports shops, and the aforementioned game arcade. Sebastian enjoyed
the inflatable castle the most, which had heated areas where there was
no shade. It was a very successful day, but my thoughts were still with
the hospital. On the way back in the car, my wife called the hospital to
ask about Natalie's condition. Fortunately, everything was fine, and
with that information, we could peacefully spend the evening.

Sunday started off beautifully. Sun rays freely entered the living
room, illuminating it with warm light. We had breakfast, but we didn't
take the little one with us. Instead, we went to the meadows behind our
house to feed the horses, and then went for a walk, taking a short break
by the pond. Ducks were swimming in the calm water, while ducks sat
on the edge, on a dark brown bench. After the break, we walked aro-
und the park and returned home, craving some hazelnut ice cream. For
the rest of the day, we stayed at home, spending time with our son.

Another day. Breakfast, train, the journey to the hospital, and riding the elevator to the appropriate floor. With smiles on our faces, we headed to the postoperative ward, eager to embrace our little daughter as soon as possible. As we entered the room, we immediately noticed that our child wasn't in her crib. Instead, we saw another family with their little one, and to make matters worse, our belongings were missing. Sebastian's book, Natalie's toys, and accessories for the little ones had all vanished. We had no clue what was happening. My hands started trembling because I disliked being in situations where we weren't informed beforehand before arriving at the hospital. After a moment, a nurse approached us and apologized for not informing us about the situation. They hadn't called us because the incident occurred about half an hour before our arrival. However, that wasn't the most important part. We didn't know where they had taken our daughter and what to expect, but if she wasn't here, nothing good could have happened to her. We were told that the child's condition had worsened again, necessitating her transfer to the ward just before intensive therapy. It was a room where infants needed careful observation. Their condition was stable enough to be there, but at any moment, one of them could be transferred to intensive care.

It could be said that Natalie's condition was fluctuating like a sine wave. Sometimes it was good, and other times it was bad. We constantly found ourselves back at square one, feeling helpless.

Gastrostomy

We cannot change anything unless we accept it.

Carl Jung

It was already the third ward since Natalie's birth to which she was transferred. If I had to choose which one was the worst, it would definitely be the intensive care unit, followed by the Children's High Dependency Unit where Natalie was, and finally, the one where she was initially placed. Our little girl was getting cramped in the infant crib, and it was clear that she had less and less space. The doctors also noticed this and suggested replacing her crib with a larger one. We agreed to it without hesitation. I should also mention that a consultant came to us and mentioned that these wards are for newborns, and Natalie was already three months old, so they would have to think about what to do with that. The machines showed an increase in oxygen flow by two units, and when the baby got upset, they increased it by four units. We didn't lose hope; we believed that our love for her was so immense that we would overcome all adversities. There was no end in sight to the fight. On the newly introduced ward, we saw some families we had seen during our time in the intensive care unit. It was heartwarming to see that some of the children had survived the toughest period.

We asked the nurse if it was possible to bathe the baby in a tub. Wiping her with wet wipes was no longer sufficient. She agreed, and after ten minutes, they brought a small bathtub, but we had to fill it with water ourselves. It was difficult to measure the water temperature by just dipping our elbows in the tub, but we managed somehow. The bigger challenge was placing the baby in the mentioned white basin. Considering how many cables Natalie was connected to, we pondered which side would be easier for us to put the tub on. The situation was complicated by the fact that the pulse and feeding cables were on one side, while the oxygen cables were on the other. Eventually, we decided to place it on the right side. We made an agreement that I would hold her while Eve would wash her. However, we couldn't do it without assistance because the oxygen cable was quite thick and heavy, causing it to constantly fall into the water. With some difficulties, we finally managed to bathe the baby properly. Previously, it was impossible as the doctors prohibited such baths and recommended cleaning the baby with special wet wipes. We wrapped her in a white towel and let her lie there for a while because we could tell she was a bit scared. However, we didn't keep her there for too long. We put on a diaper and cuddled her. Sometimes I, sometimes Eve, and Sebastian tried to entertain her with various colorful and musical toys. The baby fell asleep, and we headed towards the exit.

We felt pressure from the doctors regarding the tracheostomy. They systematically tried to persuade us at every step to sign the consent form, even though we had no intention of doing so. One time, we asked them what it would achieve besides further impairing her condition. In response, we heard that it would expedite the baby's discharge from the hospital. At times, it seemed as though they treated patients as objects rather than human beings. It's likely that the doctors we encountered had no understanding of empathy. It was all about procedures, scalpels, and goodbye.

While staying at home, we searched for all possible information that could help change the doctors' opinions. The baby had already undergone several surgeries, and we didn't want to subject her to anymore. However, after weighing all the pros and cons, we decided to go for the proposed gastrostomy. The reason for changing our decision was the fact that the nasal feeding tubes could contribute to breathing difficulties. Her nostrils were constantly congested, and this surgery could potentially help her breathe better. We were hopeful that this would be a good solution. Additionally, the nasal feeding tubes needed to be replaced every week, which caused Natalie to become even more agitated. If any of the tubes shifted or became loose, it required a visit from the machine and scanning to ensure proper placement. Furthermore, the baby was at risk of developing pressure sores internally, which we also wanted to avoid.

When we arrived at the hospital the next day, we asked the nurse for a conversation with the consultant. A tall blonde woman came and asked how she could help us. We told her everything and also inquired if the surgery could be performed as soon as possible. For the thousandth time, we heard, "Procedures, let's see what can be done." All we could do was wait. The biggest downside of this surgery was that Natalie would once again undergo general anesthesia, and each anesthesia likely leaves some trace behind.

It was Sunday, September 8th. We participated in a local race that took place in the park behind our house. Sebastian was thrilled and felt almost as good as during obstacle course races, especially because a medal awaited him at the finish line. I should also mention that the day before, there was a Parkrun event held in the same location, known worldwide, and I had consistently participated in it. That particular day was special for me because I set a new personal record and completed the challenging course of nearly five kilometers with an elevation gain of seventy-three meters in a time of twenty-six minutes and twenty-one seconds.

I was getting in better and better shape. Not only did engaging in sports allow me to momentarily forget about everything that surrounded us, but also in October, I had the Spartan Beast awaiting me—a race with obstacles where I truly needed to be well-prepared. It was another weekend when we didn't go to see Natalie. It happened to be a two-week break for me since Sebastian's summer vacation ended in early September.

We solved this by having me take Sebastian to preschool from Monday to Friday, while Eve would go to the hospital. It was a significant relief for us. This division of responsibilities greatly facilitated our daily organization.

One day, when Eve returned from Natalie and I with Sebastian were waiting on the other side of the platform to pick her up, she said that the surgery could be scheduled as early as next week. On one hand, we were happy that a date had been set, but on the other hand, we were not quite thrilled because it meant another round of tube replacements that made Natalie so anxious.

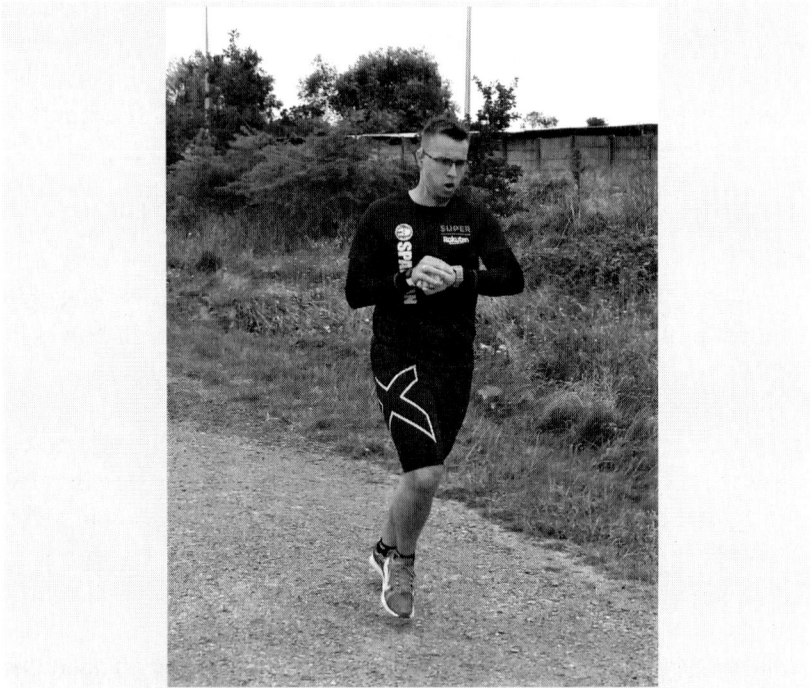

Just before the finish line, setting a new personal record during the Parkrun race

Another week passed without any changes. The surgery was performed on Friday, and we went to see Natalie on Saturday morning to ask all the questions and, of course, to cuddle our little daughter. According to the doctors' report, the operation went well without any complications. The nasal tubes were removed. Oh, how delighted we were at that sight! Only the pesky oxygen remained, but we remained hopeful that it would also disappear in due time, and we would be able to take our child home. It was evident that freeing her from the additional cables was a good decision. Natalie became calmer, and as a result, the amount of oxygen she required decreased by half. It didn't take long before another person came to us. During our hospital visits, we had encountered so many doctors and consultants that we lost track of who was responsible for what. Sometimes it even happened that someone we had already met appeared, and it felt as if we were seeing that person for the first time. This particular lady was responsible for teaching us how to properly use the gastrostomy. However, on that day, she left that task to the doctors and scheduled the training with us for the middle of the following week. We asked if it would be possible to have the training on the weekend when I could also be at the hospital because I wanted to know how to use it as well. Unfortunately, the date was non-negotiable.

The days were passing by, and my debut in obstacle course races over a distance of more than twenty-one kilometers was approaching rapidly. I didn't know how to balance everything. My preparations were going sluggishly. I was more focused on my family than on sports, but I went for runs from time to time. My goal was simply to complete the race and achieve the coveted Trifecta. I had two weeks left for preparation, but at some point, I realized it was not enough. Nevertheless, I decided to take on this challenge.

The battle between us and Natalie's doctors continued in the hospital with its gray brick walls. They pressed us in every possible way to agree to a tracheotomy. However, we remained firm in our belief to give her more time, hoping that the inflammation would pass. The child's condition fluctuated like a sine wave. We had to be prepared for anything, even for the worst. One day, my wife told me that she felt the baptism we had conducted earlier was not sufficient, and she wanted to summon a priest to the hospital. Of course, I agreed with her proposition.

On the day of the baptism, Eve went to Leeds early in the morning. Holding the child in her arms, she waited for the elderly man with a collar. The clergyman first came to the room where Natalie lay, and then together with Eve, they requested to move the child to another room where the ceremony could take place. The baptism was conducted, but only in the presence of Eve, as its date was scheduled for the only available time, on Wednesday. The day after the ceremony, the baby's condition worsened, and she came close to being connected to a ventilator again. Oxygen was increased to maximum flow, and Natalie's breathing became heavy. The little one sweated profusely, resulting in the need to change clothes twice a day. Consultations continued endlessly. We still couldn't reach an agreement. Even the doctors themselves couldn't come to a unanimous decision. Over sixty percent of the people working in the hospital and involved in Natalie's case were against a tracheotomy, while around forty percent stubbornly insisted on putting a tube in our child's throat. In the meantime, we had a conversation with the lady who specifically dealt with tracheotomy, and although she knew we wouldn't change our minds, she had to show us step by step how to take care of the child after this tragic operation. After about ten minutes, my thoughts were completely elsewhere. I wasn't listening to her, I wasn't interested in that whole dreadful thing. It was only towards the end of the conversation that she asked for my opinion. I snapped out of my thoughts and automatically replied that there was nothing to discuss. The lady tried to convince us that children with tracheotomy are happy and lead normal lives. What nonsense! One of the consultants in our initial discussions said that Natalie wasn't a child destined to die. He said that when the little girl was connected to a ventilator. He also mentioned that there were children in much worse condition on the ward. We asked him what would happen to Natalie if they disconnected all those cables and turned off the monitors right now. He didn't say anything. He fell silent and sat quietly until the end of the meeting. Everything was documented in the doctors' notes, and there was still no resolution to this matter. One time, we asked if a significant number of parents refuse the operation and disagree with the doctors' opinions. The answer was predictable, namely, a very small number of parents disagree with the operation for various reasons. However, the majority go along with it and agree to everything they are told by people in white coats.

The child's condition worsened again, but there was still no decision about connecting her to a ventilator. On a daily basis, Natalie was connected to oxygen, but when her condition deteriorated, the machine was switched to a ventilator. The doctors informed us that this could not go on for much longer, and they would have to take some action, of course, consulting with us throughout the process. After a few days, they told us that due to significant differences in medical opinions, an ethics committee would be convened to decide whether to support our stance or revoke our rights to make decisions regarding her fate. This

attempt by the doctors felt like a blow to the back. We were intimida-
ted, and warned that if the ethics committee agreed to perform a tracheotomy, we could be taken to court, and we would not be able to represent our own child. This responsibility would be assigned to a completely unrelated person who would make decisions about our daughter's life! It was unthinkable for us, but we had to arm ourselves with
patience and await the decision of the ethics committee.

Eve went to the hospital every day to be with our little girl, while I
took care of Sebastian at home. October was approaching, and there
was still no decision. Moreover, my debut in the Spartan Beast race
was getting closer, and emotionally, I was completely shattered. I wanted to be with my daughter so badly, to support her through these
difficult moments. On the other hand, I had been preparing for this race
for months and wanted to test my fighting spirit.

About a week before the trip, we were informed that a meeting of
the ethics committee had taken place. To our surprise, they informed
us that the case of our child was so challenging that they were unable
to make a final decision. Therefore, they needed the opinion of doctors
from outside Leeds.

It was the doctor specializing in throat disorders from Manchester
who arrived first. He entered the room, glanced at the monitors di-
splaying various colored numbers without even examining the child,
and after five minutes, without any hesitation, he said, "Tracheotomy."
My wife tried to present her line of reasoning, but he didn't even listen.
It seemed as if he would rather be picking his nose, eagerly waiting for
the woman next to him to stop talking so he could go and have a cup of
coffee or tea.

After several more days, a doctor specializing in the same field arrived from Sheffield. It was completely different from the first specialist. He thoroughly examined the child, listened to what my wife had to
say, and strangely enough, he agreed with her. After conducting tests,
he concluded that it would not help and that a tracheotomy would only
further deteriorate the child's condition. He also added that no one could guarantee that the tube would be removed from her throat after two
years or even after one year. The vocal cords were not functioning, and
the child was unable to breathe without machines. It was evident that

she was suffering greatly only because of the hospital procedures that were blocking her.

The opinions of both specialists were transferred to the main documentation, which was then passed on to the ethics committee.

In the midst of this situation, the worst part was the waiting. We couldn't gather our own thoughts. The fear constantly lingered in our minds that they would take our daughter away, cut her open, put her in a wheelchair, and expect her to be happy, with two tubes in her body, unable to utter a word.

While we were with Natalie, two young ladies unexpectedly approached us. They were from a children's hospice and explained to us how they operated. If the doctors' decision allowed for our child to peacefully pass away, there was the option for it to happen at their hospice instead of the hospital. However, we still had to wait for that. Just ten minutes after the two kind ladies left the room, a consultant entered to inform us that the ethics committee had made a decision, and our final consultation would take place on October 15th, with the exact time to be confirmed. They requested the presence of both parents. It was a relief that the conversation would take place after our trip. I would be able to focus on the race, and Natalie would be under the care of doctors for those few days. Sometimes it seemed like the doctors didn't understand the parents' needs, that they also needed a break from the hospital, a chance to catch their breath. We saw parents who stayed with their children day in and day out. It appeared as if they never left the premises, but in our opinion, a person should have some time for physical and mental rest.

That was the case this time as well. We only mentioned that we would be away for a few days because we had a planned trip that was scheduled even before our little one was born. They probably thought that the child was in a critical condition in the hospital, and here we were going off to have fun. Maybe they did, maybe they didn't, but we didn't care. We had also had enough of the constant fight for a better life for our little one since the moment she was born. We needed to rest, and getting away from here was highly recommended. We knew that if Natalie's condition worsened, the staff would immediately let us know. We would then come straight to the hospital, even if it meant turning around near London. We were just quietly hoping that nothing like that would happen and that we would be able to carry out our plans. We spent a little more time with our little one, and when everyone had left and we went home to pack. We had a four-hour journey ahead of us early in the morning.

Spartan Beast

C e only way to grow is by constantly raising the bar. C e only measure of success is the effort we put in to achieve it.

Bruce Lee

The morning aura didn't bode well. Instead of beautiful sunshine, it was cloudy, and there was a light wind blowing. We had packed all the necessary gear the day before and double-checked to make sure we hadn't forgotten anything. Fortunately, everything was in order, and after a hearty breakfast, we set off for the town of Reading, which was about a thirty-minute drive from the event location. We decided to book a hotel the day before because I preferred to get a good night's sleep on the day of the race. There have been times when we left on the same day between five and six in the morning when the race started at ten. It was exhausting, but luckily the distances to run were short. This time, we were facing over four hours of driving, so I couldn't imagine spending that much time behind the wheel and then running over twenty kilometers. Turning the key in the door, I glanced out the window to check if we had turned off all the lights. I started the car, and we hit the road.

While driving on the highway, I occasionally glanced at my wife. It was evident that she couldn't stop thinking about Natalie. Especially since we had the final consultation ahead, and we had no idea how our daughter's fate would unfold. However, I tried to approach this trip in a way that would keep us as far away from the hospital as possible and avoid bringing up the topic altogether.

After over four hours of exhausting driving, we arrived at the hotel. We met up with friends who were also participating in the sporting event, and then we went to sleep.

The next day, I woke up earlier than Eve and Sebastian. I needed to have a light meal so that I could leave calmly afterward. Since I was completely unfamiliar with the area, I set the GPS to the destination and we calmly made our way there.

As we entered the event area, I parked the car in the spot indicated by a volunteer wearing sunglasses and a yellow reflective vest. I decided to change into the clothes I planned to run in right away. There was no point in leaving the bag with all my belongings in the paid locker room when I could leave everything in the trunk. We put rain boots on Sebastian since the area was fertile and mostly muddy, and then we headed toward the registration area.

Despite the early hour, the queue was already quite long, and it took me over half an hour to show my ID and collect my race number along with the timing chip under the black tent.

Eve and our son settled on a picnic blanket near the coffee stand, while I went with my friends near the starting line to see the first wave of professionals, the Elite wave, in which some of my acquaintances were participating. With loud applause, I began cheering on all the participants right after the final countdown. Everyone shot forward, and it didn't take long before they disappeared around the corner, running into the forest.

It was the men's start. This is how every race begins, and after a short break, the next wave of professionals entered the starting line, this time the women. From a guy's perspective, there was plenty to admire, with fit female figures catching the eye. Fortunately, I had already found the one for me, so all that was left was to cheer and encourage them to give their best right after the countdown. They ran off and disappeared into the forest just as quickly as their male counterparts.

Every now and then, I approached my family and asked how they were doing. Fortunately, they were fine, just tired. Overall, my wife didn't enjoy attending such events with Sebastian due to his restlessness. It was the same this time; he couldn't sit still and was constantly dissatisfied with something. His greatest joy came from approaching the starting line and cheering on his dad. With such supportive fans, I always entered the race with great pride.

My wave was scheduled to start at 11 o'clock, so I still had plenty of time to warm up properly and mentally prepare myself before this challenge.

*Happy after completing the twenty-three-kilometer route, which was in-
tended to be two kilometers shorter*

The time had come. They called everyone to the starting line, and the race officials turned on motivational music. There were a lot of us, not to mention the people who had started running ahead of us. The most important thing was to avoid creating queues at the obstacles. Howeve-ver, I had no illusions about such a large number of runners. There was a high probability that we would have to wait a while before the ob-stacles.

The countdown began, and I couldn't wait to finally disappear aro-und the corner, following in the footsteps of those who went before me. I was excited to see how the course would unfold and, of course, if I would be able to finish the race at all. We started. Some shot off like a slingshot, while others took it easy, pacing themselves for the entire distance. Personally, I belonged to the latter group. I preferred to start calmly because, honestly, I didn't know how to distribute my energy. I overcame the first obstacle and then entered the forest, following the path marked by taped boundaries. The deeper into the woods, the more branches littered the trail. I had to be very careful. I kept running, facing each obstacle that came my way. Sometimes I succeeded, and other times I had to do penalty burpees. During the race, I was able to calm my mind and forget about the daily problems surrounding me. I liked that. Having a clear mind was crucial at that moment. I completed the course at my own pace. I wasn't in a hurry; my only concern was to cross the finish line. Finally, after four hours, forty-seven minutes, and seventeen hundredths, I achieved my goal. I crossed the finish line, feeling as happy as a child with a toy. I was thrilled that I had managed to achieve this goal and complete the trifecta!

The final piece of the puzzle has been completed

Finally, it dawned on me that it was time to return to reality. Thoughts and everything related to the matter came rushing back. In a few days, we were facing the final consultation, and we had no idea what decision the doctors would make.

In the days leading up to the conversation, Eve had been going to the hospital and telling me about how unwell our little one was. She was constantly hooked up to various colored cables, and the oxygen was flowing at maximum settings. The doctors said they were trying to decrease the oxygen levels periodically, but soon after, they had to return to the highest settings because the child couldn't cope. The decision about whether to use the ventilator again had not yet been made.

Finally, the day arrived. I had never been so stressed in my life. My hands were trembling. Mentally, I was somewhere else on the way to the hospital. I didn't know if this horror would finally come to an end or if it would continue, and we would have to navigate through courts, unable to even represent our own child. We wanted it to be over. While being with our little one, I occasionally glanced at the clock's hands, and despite the machines beeping around me, I imagined hearing the ticking sound. I held the tiny baby in my arms, crying all the while, and repeating to her that no matter what happens, I love her with all my heart. That I will do everything in my power to prevent her from suffering any longer, from being cut and treated like an object. The pain she had endured since birth had been more than enough.

The hour of the court arrived. We were invited into the room, and once again, we were offered coffee and cookies filled to the brim with cream. Without hesitation, we turned on our son's cartoons and let him watch whatever he liked, even those that we didn't particularly enjoy or consider suitable for children. We wanted to focus on the conversation. Before everyone took their seats, I asked someone sitting across from us to hand Eve a whole pack of tissues because I knew tears would be inevitable.

We were once again presented with Natalie's story, and then we were told that medical ethics aligned with our opinion and that a tracheostomy would not help in her case. The child would be condemned to a vegetative state, suffering for the rest of her life. According to the ethics committee, Natalie's case was one in ten thousand. The spina bifida itself wasn't as severe as the complications the child had developed in the days following her birth. Such complications had never been seen before in that hospital. Everyone agreed that it was best to let the child pass away peacefully, to end her suffering. We were only asked where we would like all the machines to be disconnected so that we could say our final goodbyes to our little angel in peace and quiet, while the staff took care of Sebastian.

Everyone was looking at us, and we remained silent for a while, unable to hold back our tears. They waited for us to respond. After wiping our eyes, we simply said, "Thank you." Initially, we wanted the farewell to take place in the same hospital, but after speaking with a doctor working at a children's hospice, we were convinced that the entire process should take place there. We made this decision because we were told that it is a more pleasant, cozy, and peaceful environment compared to the place we had been going to for the past few months.

The gathered people left the room, saying they would give us a moment of privacy to talk. After about five minutes, we stood up from the couch, finishing the last sip of cold coffee because there was nothing more to discuss. We simply embraced each other, reassuring ourselves that we had done everything in our power to save her. However, we had to say "enough" and let go.

We returned to our little one. She wasn't sleeping. I looked deep into her eyes and told her that I love her very much and she will always remain in my heart. I didn't even sit on a chair, just sat on the floor and curled up, still crying. I felt helpless. Doctors kept coming up to me every now and then, asking if I needed anything if they could bring me water or give me a calming pill. All I wanted was for everyone to leave me alone. Even now, as I write this passage, tears well up in my eyes. I don't want to hold them back. But when we left the hospital, we kissed Natalie, everyone saying she was our little angel. I was in such a state that I didn't even pay attention to the surroundings or to the other parents who were probably looking at us the whole time.

We finally calmed down after some time and decided it was time to go home. But before leaving the hospital, the doctor from the hospice informed us that Eve should come to the hospital early tomorrow morning, and they would arrange for her and Natalie to be transported by ambulance to the facility. Around 9 o'clock, the transportation would take place. As for me, I had to first drop off Sebastian at preschool, then pick him up, and only then go to the hospice. When I picked up my son from preschool, I approached his teacher and asked if I could talk to her in a separate room. Once in the room, I explained to her why Sebastian wouldn't be attending preschool for an indefinite period. A tear rolled down my cheek as I spoke.

When I picked up my son, the phone rang. It was one of the staff members from the hospice, urging me to come as soon as possible.

They emphasized that I should drive slowly and cautiously.

ℋospice

You can pray for a miracle, but you shouldn't expect one. Miracles do not happen on demand, nor can they be demanded from the Lord God.

Priest John Kaczkowski

I packed a suitcase, although not a big one. I had no idea how long we would be there or how things would unfold. I put my son in the car seat, set up the navigation, and set off to reach our destination as quickly as possible. I drove cautiously, following the instructions of the lady who called me earlier. I knew I had to focus on the road, especially since I had my son with me. It was my first time driving this route, and in a way, I was curious about what the hospice would look like.

After about forty minutes, a building with an open entrance gate came into view, revealing a parking lot full of cars beyond it. Seeing people walking by, I rolled down the window and asked if I had arrived at the right place. Upon receiving a positive response, I turned left to find a parking spot. It was only at the very end that I managed to park the car, grab my son, and quickly make our way to the reception without even taking any luggage. After pressing the intercom, a lady answered, asking who I was visiting. I replied that today I brought my daughter Natalie and her mother here, as instructed, and was asked to come as soon as possible. We were let inside, and one of the staff members led us to our destination. We walked through a narrow corridor, with entrances to rooms on both the left and right sides. We passed a music hall and then entered a sensory room, where it was almost completely dark. Lights on the walls illuminated, constantly changing their shape and color. Eve was sitting on the floor, holding Natalie, who was intensely captivated by the mesmerizing lights. A portable oxygen machine was constantly connected to our daughter, and in the room, apart from the hospice doctor and us, there was also the ambulance driver and a

99

nurse who was on duty that day, responsible for accompanying the little one and required to come to the hospice along with Eve from the hospital in Leeds. Sebastian also enjoyed the colorful patterns. It was good that our son found something of interest, allowing us to focus on the final farewell. We cried, not knowing when they would remove all the cables from her. We wanted her to see the blue sky and trees at least once, so we asked for a wheelchair and to take her outside to the garden on the facility grounds. They brought us a pushchair, in which Natalie barely fit, and we walked towards the exit. We sat on a bench while a caregiver was asked to watch over Sebastian. He was taken care of by a young hospice volunteer. She showed him a shed in the garden where there were worn-out and tattered toys, with only a few suitable for play. She didn't take him inside the facility because Sebastian wanted to have his parents in sight. It was a new place, new people, and he was a bit scared. He was too young to understand what was happening at that moment.

There was silence and a light; a cool breeze was blowing. The silence was interrupted by the hospice doctor asking if we were ready. The child was on diazepam and morphine to prevent any pain. We replied that we were ready. We wanted it to happen at that moment when we felt that we had done everything in our power to save her. We had fought for her day in and day out for the past few months, and we had a clear conscience. The ambulance driver gently removed the oxygen from her nose and disconnected all the machines. The child looked at the gently swaying autumn leaves. We asked how long it would take, but unfortunately, no one knew the answer. Once again, we heard that it depended on the child, but looking at the readings from the machines connected to her, it could be assumed that it shouldn't take long. We stayed by her side the whole time, waiting for the worst, but nothing happened. We sat there with her for another two hours, and the child continued to observe the yellow-orange leaves on the tree. Her diaper was already full, and we were disoriented. What really happened there? All we could do was wait, and I glanced at Sebastian from the corner of my eye, seeing him playing with a toy with the caregiver. It was a yellow, plastic excavator with a broken black arm in one place.

The doctor said that she would leave us alone with one of the hospice workers as she needed to go fill out some paperwork. It was getting chilly, so I went back to the nearby room that was heated from the inside, and Eve put the baby down in the stroller, closely observing what was happening. The little girl lay there, continuously staring at one spot, occasionally glancing at her mother.

One of the trees on the grounds of the facility was also being observed by Natalie

After some time, we asked the kind lady if she could call the doctor for us because we didn't know whether we should just sit there or return to the room. The doctor came shortly after, completely unaware of such a turn of events. She asked us to accompany her to the center.

There, she explained to us that they would continue to monitor the child, administer medications, and if anything were to happen, they would inform us immediately. Now they invited us to have a warm meal as the cafeteria had just opened. Natalie was also looking at a tree on the premises. We were delighted to see Natalie without the machines, but we approached everything with great caution. We saw the state she was in at the hospital, and the numbers spoke for themselves. We left our little one under the care of a nurse and finally went to eat after all the emotions that accompanied us since the last consultation. The food was delicious. I didn't expect it to taste so exquisite. After a hearty meal, we went to sit in the lounge, which was connected to the area where the kitchen tables were set up. There was a large television in the middle with a DVD player, and children in various conditions were watching cartoons.

We took a moment to rest, sitting on a very comfortable sofa where one could easily fall asleep. There were other people milling around. We needed this break, even if just for a moment, but we knew we had to return to the room because our daughter's fate was uncertain. Walking down the same corridor towards the room as we did at the beginning of our visit to the hospice, we passed people along the way whose expressions indicated that something terrible must have happened in their case. I turned the doorknob, we entered the room, and we saw that our little one had fallen asleep while being watched over by one of the staff members. We had a brief conversation with her and then went outside to enjoy the nice weather. We transferred Natalie, along with her monitoring device, into a stroller, and together with Sebastian, we sat on brown wooden chairs by comfortable coffee tables. A gentle breeze blew away the steam from our coffees, and our son enjoyed freshly made toast with raspberry jam. We also had to shoo away a wasp that was tempted by the sweet scent of the fruit.

As Natalie received regular doses of medication to alleviate her pain, I wondered if she was even aware of anything. One thing was certain: the peculiar sound she made didn't disappear. Natalie continued to produce a sound resembling a rooster's crow, yet she was able to breathe on her own. The doctors were baffled. We were only informed about the time limit for staying at the facility and that they would assist us with all the necessary formalities regarding our child's passing. However, now they began preparing a Plan B, and we were kept updated on the developments.

The first night in the hospice was terrible; we hardly got any sleep. We had to call the nurse every moment because Natalie was crying constantly. To calm her down, we administered oral morphine. It had a faster effect compared to the one given through the gastrostomy tube.

In the morning, despite the freezing weather, rays of sunshine entered our room. We got up feeling tired, changed Natalie's diaper, and then headed to breakfast. Our meal was interrupted by the doctor, who asked us to go to the small room behind the couch in the living room after breakfast.

When we opened the door, our eyes were greeted by a wall on the right side, painted with a huge rainbow from floor to ceiling, adorned with thousands of tiny photos. As I approached the wall to examine them more closely, I noticed pictures of children. They were individuals who had been at the hospice since its establishment. I could never have imagined that so many infants and young people had been in contact with this place. My attention was diverted from the colorful wall by a woman's voice. The doctor said that no one had anticipated such a turn of events, so they would monitor Natalie, and if everything went well, they would transport our daughter to Wakefield Hospital by the end of the week or in the following week to teach us how to properly use the gastrostomy. She also added that anything could happen; for now, Natalie was doing well, but her condition could change dramatically, just as it had in the hospital before. We acknowledged all the information, dressed Natalie, and headed towards the tiny church located in the garden. We walked along a small path paved with various shades of gray pebbles. In the distance, we could see gray rabbits. There were quite a few of them. We entered the small building, but before we began to pray, the priest arrived. We told him the whole story about our daughter, and together we recited the Lord's Prayer. In the room, one wall was entirely made of glass, and through the windows, we could see more groups of rabbits hopping on the grass lightly covered with dew. They seemed accustomed to this place. As we stepped back outside, we took a closer look at the entire garden. Ribbons were tied to the trees, presumably symbolizing the people who had passed away here. If our daughter had also closed her eyes here forever, they would probably have attached another ribbon. Fortunately, that didn't happen, just as we declined the offer of having Natalie's photo hanging on the rainbow wall after careful consideration.

We already knew that we would have to stay at the hospice longer than we initially thought, so I packed a bag with dirty clothes and took it home. I left early in the morning to have enough time to clean the house, do the laundry, pack clean clothes, and return to my family. However, I asked them to make sure to call me if anything happened.

While cleaning the house, I heard a notification on my phone. It turned out to be a message from an acquaintance offering to send me a Saint Charbel oil from Poland. She explained its uses and emphasized the importance of saying a heartfelt prayer while applying it to the child. I read the message, and thanked her, but declined the offer. I wasn't convinced about such oils and simply disregarded the matter.

When the sun began to set, I headed to the facility. The journey was just as safe as the previous time, with the only difference being that I could park the car right in front of the main entrance since there were fewer visitors at that hour, and the parking spaces were almost empty.

As I entered the room, our daughter was still sleeping, continuously making that unpleasant sound.

I was so exhausted by that day that after dinner, I simply went to sleep and only woke up around eight in the morning. Apparently, my body needed that rest. My wife and children were still sleeping, so I went to the kitchen to make myself some coffee. I comfortably sat on the couch, and gradually, people from the hospice started gathering in the kitchen. Parents with their little ones and caregivers. Within an hour, they occupied almost all the tables. As I sat there, sipping my hot beverage, once again, it struck me that we were not the only ones facing serious challenges related to our child.

As I was putting down my cup, I noticed my family entering the room. Eve left the stroller for me, and she and our son went to have breakfast. I started making funny faces to amuse Natalka in the stroller, closely observing her reactions. Despite being on medication, she smiled when she saw her dad making silly expressions. It was a good sign that things were starting to go in the right direction.

After breakfast, we went for a walk. We strolled through the park, discovering new pathways and enjoying the surroundings. When we returned to the building, we learned that soon a lady with animals would be visiting as part of a special therapy session. All the children eagerly awaited the visit, peering through the glass doors. When she arrived, we sat down to take advantage of this unique opportunity. The woman carefully placed a rabbit in Natalie's stroller and gave Sebastian a guinea pig, first spreading a cloth with a small amount of sawdust on our laps. It was clear that this kind of attraction brought a lot of joy to the children. After two hours, the owner of all the pets left the facility, and we headed to the playroom. As we sat on the floor, another lady approached us. At first, I thought she was another doctor who would start talking to us about procedures, medications, and hospitals, but she turned out to be an artist. After a moment, I noticed a large piece of white canvas behind her bag. She asked us if we would like to press Natalie's little feet on the canvas, and then she would turn it into a tree as a memento for us to have something nice from this place. We agreed, and after a while, we took off the baby's socks, and the lovely lady brought dark brown paint. The baby's feet hardly moved. Firstly, the doctors had told us that with a spinal cleft, there was a high probability of mobility issues or complete paralysis of the legs. The first foot was covered in paint, and the artist gently pressed it against the canvas. Suddenly, the baby kicked her leg vigorously, leaving behind three brown streaks. We fell silent because no one expected that to happen. Instead of a print of the foot, there were brown streaks. The elderly lady reassured us not to worry about it. After a moment, she took Natalie's feet again, first one, then the other, and this time she successfully imprinted the little feet. The next step was for her to paint the trunk of the tree without leaves because our imprinted hands were supposed to serve as the leaves. It was already late, so we postponed these last two steps to the following day.

The next day, we had some formalities to take care of regarding Natalie's transportation to the hospital, but not all of them required our presence. So we left Sebastian with the caregiver and went home to clean up and bring fresh clothes. As we were returning home, we remembered the painting that we were supposed to finish. Well, we quietly hoped that the artist would show up again and allow us to complete the artwork.

As soon as we arrived at our destination, the first thing I did was prepare water for my favorite coffee. I was feeling tired, and there was still the journey back ahead of me. After taking the last sip, I went to help my wife with cleaning and packing our clothes. We managed to finish everything quite quickly, as it took us no more than three hours. Then we set off on our way back. While I was driving, Eve asked me if our little one would manage. Without thinking too long, I replied that I think she would. She laughed at me yesterday after they disconnected her from the machines, didn't she? One thing I was certain of: we needed to stay positive and hopeful until the very end.

When we arrived at the place, Sebastian was busy playing with the caregiver, and it was only when we called him that he came running to hug us. Natalie was sleeping nearby in her stroller.

Exhausted after the whole day, we went to sleep because we didn't know what the next day would bring us.

The next day, we received information about transporting Natalie to the hospital in Wakefield. We were very happy that everything was starting to go in the right direction, and we almost forgot about the unfinished painting. Luckily, the artist was at the hospice that day, so we managed to bring the unfinished painting to the studio. There were connected tables with chairs placed around them, and antique furniture stood around. Paints and other tools for creating artwork were scattered on them. We were interested in various shades of green, which I soon noticed on one desk. We all painted our hands with ink and gently pressed our hands onto the canvas, thus creating a magnificent and unique painting.

Even then, I knew that this painting would hang in our home, in the kitchen, as the most precious artifact symbolizing the difficult journey we had to go through.

We had just brought clean clothes, and already we had to pack them back again because the transportation of the child was scheduled for the next day, around nine o'clock in the morning.

In the meantime, someone knocked on our door. It was a musician, an older man with gray hair, who asked if we would like to go to the music hall and listen to the beautiful pieces he could play for us. We decided that it would be a good idea to have some entertainment and music for the children. We entered the hall, where almost every instrument was present - a piano, drums, flute, guitars, microphones, and so on. The kind man tuned one of the guitars and then sat as close as possible to the stroller where Natalie was lying, and he began to play. The little girl stared at the instrument with her beautiful blue eyes.

A canvas painting created in the hospice

We said goodbye to all the caregivers at the facility, thanking them for the warm welcome and care they provided for Natalie, and we wished them all the best.

In the morning, while everyone was still asleep, I started packing all our belongings into the car. I wrapped the painting in a towel to ensure it wouldn't get damaged. The ambulance had a delay, but fortunately, it wasn't too long. The planned departure was around nine o'clock, and after taking care of all the formalities, the departure was delayed by less than an hour.

Eve went with Natalie in the ambulance, while Sebastian and I took our car. As I drove out of the parking lot, I turned left, leaving behind the gray walls of the facility with the thought of never returning there again.

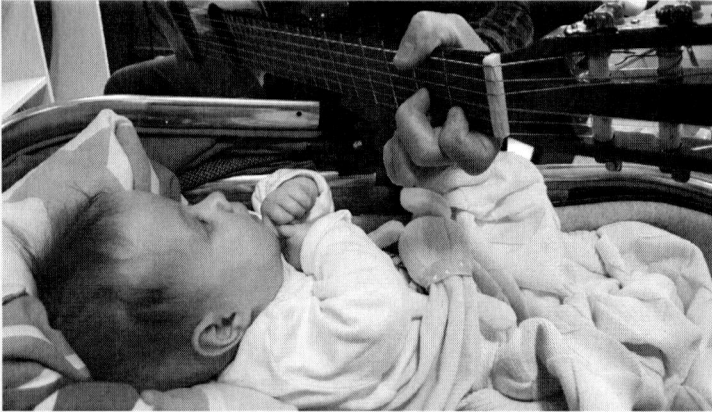

The music hall and music therapy

The GPS guided me on a different route than the one the ambulance took, but we were still supposed to meet at the same location, so the choice of route didn't matter that much. I entered the highway, where there was heavy traffic. I drove calmly, focusing on reaching our destination safely. We weren't in a hurry, so I had plenty of time for reflection and analyzing the entire situation at the hospice. Everything unfolded differently than what we were told, and somewhere in the back of my mind, I began searching for a rational explanation, but I couldn't find one. How did it happen that all the numbers indicated the child's critical condition, yet after the machines were disconnected, the child was still alive? There was no scientific explanation for this; it was undoubtedly the work of a higher power.

The journey to the hospital took me less than an hour. I parked the car at the front of the parking lot, fortunate enough to find someone leaving at that moment. Sebastian had fallen asleep, and carrying him from the far end of the vast parking lot wouldn't be easy. I lifted him onto my shoulders and made my way towards the entrance, passing people in hospital gowns with IV drips, some of them smoking cigarettes. I took the elevator to the highest floor where the ward was located, where Natalie was supposed to be transferred. I rang the intercom, explaining the purpose of my visit, and then closed the door behind me.

Hospital

Success is the sum of small efforts, repeated day in and day out.

Robert Collier

Heading towards the reception, I passed by a corner for parents where they could prepare coffee or tea. Then I walked past a few rooms and reached the reception, which was located to the right of them. I politely introduced myself and asked which room my daughter, who arrived here with her mother from the children's hospice, was assigned to. The receptionist looked into the system and said that nobody had arrived yet, and they were still waiting.

I didn't expect us to arrive earlier. We left at the same time. Apparently, the route I took with my son turned out to be much shorter because it also took me some time to get from the parking lot to the hospital.

I didn't have to wait long. It was literally a moment, and I saw my wife with Natalie and the ambulance driver heading towards the reception. When my wife asked which room we should go to, the receptionist pointed to a room across from us. We entered the room, and I started slowly carrying the most essential items from the car, planning to take the less necessary ones home later in the evening.

The hospital room was quite spacious, with its own bathroom, so accommodating four people plus occasional hospital staff was not a problem. While I was unpacking Eve's suitcase, the doctor entered and announced that she would come back in about an hour to explain everything to us. This would include procedures, the expected duration of our stay, and what we would be taught. We had a rough idea of the whole situation, but it never hurts to hear it again.

While waiting for the doctor, we hung the image of St. Sharbel on

the hospital bed, and we placed her necklace on the shelf. It was enclo-
sed in blue packaging symbolizing her guardian angel. While still at
the hospice, I asked my acquaintance to send us the holy oil after all.
We had nothing to lose. The condition of the little one was improving
day by day, but the voice resembling a rooster's crow had not disappeared, so we had to remain vigilant and prepared for any circumstances.

The time came when a couple of people entered the room, and we
began to guess their respective specializations. Firstly, we were presented with the hundredth rendition of the medical history, and then
they explained that we were here to learn how to use the gastrostomy,
and once we mastered the procedure, we would be discharged home.
We would be assigned a primary care doctor and a rehabilitation specialist to monitor our child's progress regularly. The conversation lasted for about an hour, and afterward, we left our little one under the
care of a nurse and finally went to eat something.

It was slowly getting dark, and I could see that Sebastian was tired.
So, we said goodbye to our girls and headed home. As we passed the
hospital on the right side, I told my son to wave and that we would
come back there tomorrow. It didn't take even five minutes for him to
fall asleep.

Upon arriving home, I put him to bed and started cleaning. I prepared the laundry that I intended to put in the washing machine early the
next morning so that it wouldn't run during the night. I finished cleaning around two in the morning. I went to bed because the next day
promised to be eventful as well. I couldn't wait for the whole family to
return home, but I knew I had to be patient a little while longer.

After picking up our son from preschool, we headed to our girls.
Nothing had changed at the hospital; nurses would come to the room
regularly to replace milk bags and administer medication. This routine
went on for a few days. Every day, Sebastian and I would visit Eve and
Natalie until one of the doctors informed us that the next day we would
begin training on how to use the gastrostomy. We were eager for any
progress because we were getting tired of the same routine. With the
good news that they would finally show us how to feed her, I made my
way back home. It was quite late as the hospital visit ended later than
usual. As I opened the door, I nearly stepped on an envelope lying on

the doormat. Inside the envelope, there was a vial of holy oil and a few incense sticks. I thanked God that the letter from Poland arrived so quickly. I only wrote to my wife, letting her know that we had safely arrived home.

On the last evening, to make sure I didn't forget the oil, I immediately put the vial into my backpack. I was very curious about my wife's reaction when she saw the item. We arrived at the hospital and went straight to the room to greet the girls. Additionally, we brought a warm meal because the prices at the hospital were very high. It cost over five pounds for just one person's lunch, and the food there was not tasty at all.

Before taking out the oil from my backpack, I asked Eve if anyone had come to show her how to use the gastrostomy tube. She told me that no one had come yet, but someone was supposed to arrive soon.

Unzipping the smallest pocket of my backpack, I took out the oil and showed it to my wife. She was very happy that it had arrived so quickly and couldn't wait to say a prayer and anoint Natalie with it in the areas that had been most affected since birth, especially her vocal cords, as they posed the biggest challenge. I asked Eve to go to the reception and inquire about the time someone would come to administer her medications and feed, as I didn't want anyone entering our room during the prayer. The prayer had to flow from the depths of our hearts, and any interruption would disrupt the whole plan.

We closed the curtains and asked not to be disturbed for at least thirty minutes, as we wanted to pray. The information was acknowledged by the receptionist, and the time of the request was noted down.

We carefully took out the vial of oil from the bag, making sure not to drop it. It would have been a tragedy to lose such a valuable item! Our son was too young to participate in the prayer, which had to be conducted straight from the heart. To prevent him from (as strange as it may sound) disturbing us, we turned on his favorite cartoon for him. Thankfully, he sat quietly in his chair, allowing us to proceed with the ritual. We had the prayer printed on a piece of paper. We began reading it shortly after placing the vial back into the bag. The prayer flowed from our hearts, and we didn't even look at each other, just at our little one, waiting to see what would happen. I had always been skeptical about such prayers. This time, there was nothing left for us but to believe that her vocal cords would start working. After finishing the prayer, nothing changed. We observed, or rather listened if her wheezing during breathing would subside. No change. The child continued to make the sound that haunted our nights. Feeling disheartened, I said goodbye to my wife and returned home with our son. During the journey back, I kept thinking, why didn't it work? Why do we exert all our efforts, yet the results are meager? I had no answer to that question. I felt sorry that there was nothing more I could do, and in the back of my mind lingered the thought, what if her condition worsens? With a mind full of thoughts, I went to sleep.

The next morning started just like the previous ones. We got dressed, prepared breakfast, and then headed to the hospital, stopping on the way to refuel the car. After parking in the last aisle of the hospital parking lot and pressing the lock button on the key, we made our way with our son toward the entrance of the building. Along the way, we passed people in white robes smoking their cigarettes. We went through the revolving doors, but before we could take the elevator to the upper floor, my son insisted on getting the latest newspaper about building blocks from the kiosk on the first floor. I bought it for him, not paying any attention to the fact that I was making a mistake by giving in to his every desire. I was already tired, and my thoughts were wandering far away.

Entering the room, I saw our daughter sleeping in her crib, but I didn't see my wife. Either she went downstairs to get something to eat or she went to the bathroom. It didn't take five minutes before my wife returned to the room with a warm meal, but instead of greeting me, she smiled widely. Her eyes were fixed on mine, not even blinking. I didn't know what to say or rather, what to ask, as she hadn't uttered a single word yet. About thirty seconds passed, and then Eve said that the dreadful wheezing during breathing had disappeared! Our prayers had been answered, and I sat down on a chair, not knowing what to say. At first, I couldn't believe it, but we did it! The oil worked!

While waiting for Eve, I didn't even notice that Natalie was sleeping so peacefully. Today, the doctors were supposed to come again, but they didn't specify the exact time. I needed a moment to process all these wonderful new pieces of information in my mind.

Does a higher power exist? I did not know the answer to this question, but judging by recent events, I could surmise that someone, or rather something, has been watching over us, especially over Natalie since her birth.

My wife, throwing away the plastic packaging from breakfast, glanced at sleeping Natalie and couldn't take her eyes off her. A smile returned to her face. The thought that there is a lot of hard work ahead of us still lingered in the back of her mind. However, now we wanted to focus on getting trained in handling the gastrostomy as quickly as possible and getting discharged to go home. After all, this little one has never seen her own home!

Hours passed, and the doctors were still nowhere to be seen. We had grown accustomed to this, so all we could do was wait. In the meantime, I went downstairs to have some lunch. I knew it would come at a high cost, but there was no possibility of preparing a meal in the morning. I don't remember exactly what I ordered, but it was probably French fries with beans and eggs. There wasn't much variety, but I had to eat something. I had my meal at the cafeteria because I knew the children were being taken care of by their mother. After swallowing the last bite, I pushed my chair back and made my way toward the elevator, stopping by a kiosk on the way to get some sweets and drinks.

The elevator doors closed, and I arrived on the second floor. This time, I was allowed in without being asked about the purpose of my visit.

When I entered the room, I saw doctors talking to my wife. After a while, one of the doctors greeted me and informed me that they had arrived recently and were having a discussion for about ten minutes. I introduced myself and then went to see what my son was doing, or rather, what cartoon he was watching. Fortunately, there was a nice cartoon about a pink pig in a red skirt playing.

The only ones missing in the room were the physiotherapists who were supposed to come and ask about Natalie. People in the room were speculating about her future, completely disregarding the medications she was on at the time. Some of them were direct and blunt, mentioning that my daughter may have mobility problems in the future, and the speech therapist emphasized that she may not be able to speak or articulate most words. However, it seemed that nobody took into account that the child is very young and is being administered strong medications such as morphine or diazepam, powerful psychotropic drugs. Everyone present presented the situation to us clearly, explaining what the care for the little one would look like, and then each went their own way. However, they didn't mention what we had been waiting for several days: when someone would finally train us on how to handle this damn gastrostomy? It was becoming truly frustrating. The constant brushing off often made us feel like we were being neglected by them. It was only later that someone informed us that the hospital was short-staffed, and that's why everything was taking so long, but they would try to organize the appropriate personnel as soon as possible to train us in feeding the child. From time to time, we observed how the nurse did it, where she heated the food, and what doses she used. However, it wasn't the kind of learning we needed, especially since initially she was supposed to receive overnight nutrition through a machine that automatically dispenses the food.

That machine was supposed to be delivered to our home. In the near future, a delivery date was supposed to be determined. The only question that arose was, what does "in the near future" mean to them? A few days, a week, two weeks, a month? It was another unknown that we had to live with.

The days continued to pass without any changes, but after a week, we were finally informed that the next day we would begin the training on operating the machine and handling the gastrostomy. In the meantime, all the necessary equipment was delivered to our home. We truly couldn't wait for this ordeal to be over.

It was getting colder, and October was clearly showing that the frost was slowly approaching. However, feeling a slight tingling on my nose and cheeks due to the temperature, I reached into the car's glove compartment for the window defroster because it was so cold overnight that the windows had managed to freeze. While the car's heating supported me in the battle against the frozen windows, I put my son in the car seat, and when visibility was very good, we set off once again on the same route, passing a traffic jam caused by roadworks along the way.

My daughter was already awake, and when we entered the room, I saw a smile on her face. She smiled upon seeing a familiar person, and her little blue eyes stared at me as I walked to the other side of the hospital bed. Despite being on strong medication, she could recognize the people closest to her. Dressed in shorts and a little blouse, she continued to gaze at me for about five more minutes, and I couldn't stop listening to her soft breath and noticing that her hair was getting lighter, transitioning from black to a straw-blond shade, just like my wife's hair.

Our training began in the afternoon. On the first day, we had to pour the milk into the machine ourselves and learn how to administer it. It wasn't as difficult as it initially seemed, although Natalie wasn't going to be discharged from the hospital until the doctors were certain that we would be able to handle the administration once we were at home. The biggest challenge was ensuring that the milk, which we had to warm up, wasn't too hot or too cold. There were times when we had to discard it and prepare a new batch.

The practice was going well. Every time I returned home, I tried to take as many things as possible so that after the discharge, I could just come back for them and take as little luggage as possible.

The nurses closely observed how we managed on our own. They would occasionally point out when we made mistakes because we couldn't afford to make such errors at home. Meanwhile, the physiotherapists brought a blue seat into the room. They wanted to see how Natalie would handle it so that she wouldn't have to lie in bed all the time. They didn't want pressure sores to develop. There was already a tiny mark on her knee, so they were determined to avoid it at all costs. One of the physiotherapists took the child and gently placed her in the seat, then adjusted the safety belts.

Natalie took a liking to the new position right from the start. Her balance was still a work in progress, and her head would tilt to the side. However, we were confident that she would manage and gradually develop her posture, strengthening all her muscles. Everything was starting to fall into place, and even the cooler days no longer had a negative impact on our well-being.

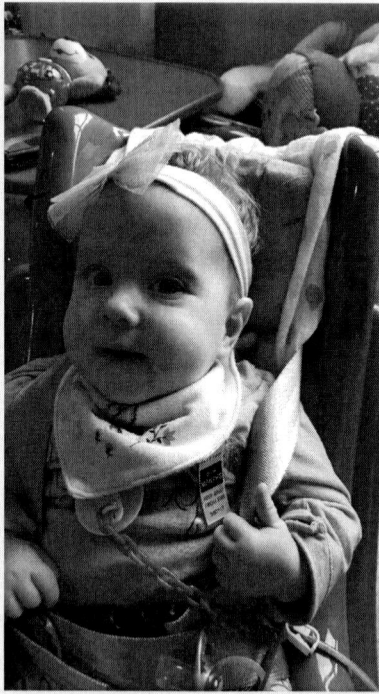

Natalie in the chair

Our return home was getting closer and closer, but there were still a few formalities left to take care of. If everything went according to plan, we would be discharged with the medications and a schedule on how to administer them. The girl was still on morphine and diazepam. The treatment plan involved gradually reducing the medication doses each week while closely monitoring the child's condition. We had come so far that we couldn't give up or look back. However, at the back of our minds, we couldn't erase the thought that things could change, and the child's condition could deteriorate again.

No one knew how the little one would function after weaning off the medications. All we had left was faith that everything would turn out well for her.

In the room, there was nothing left of our personal belongings except for one backpack and a pack of diapers. Everything had been previously taken home because the long-awaited day had finally arrived—the day when we would discharge the child and bring her home! The final paperwork was packed in a folder, and my wife dressed Natalie before gently placing her in the car seat. The little girl was wearing a bright pink jacket with various flower patterns, and she had a warm, gray hat with a pom-pom on her head. She looked at me with her beautiful, blue eyes while sucking on a pacifier attached to a small, red chain.

Natalie just before leaving the hospital

We thanked the staff at the reception and then closed the door to the children's ward behind us. We took the elevator down and made our way toward the main entrance. As we stepped outside, a chilly wind blew. It was morning, and clouds moved across the sky, occasionally revealing half of the moon. The hospital parking lot was much larger compared to the one at the children's hospital in Leeds. I parked our car, probably in row F, as there was no space available in the front. The windows had already frozen over. I took Natalie and gently placed the car seat on the back seat. We turned on the heating, and once the visibility was good, we set off on our journey back home.

As we arrived in our hometown, we had to make a stop at the pharmacy to get the necessary medications and supplies for Natalie's gastrostomy care. We also picked up four heavy packages of special food for her. Fortunately, the pharmacy order fit into the trunk, where the last bags from the hospital were placed. I closed the trunk gently, making sure not to break any glass, and then we set off for home.

I turned the key in the ignition as I parked near our house and thought to myself, "Finally, it's over." We did it! After months of hard struggle, our little girl will finally see her home for the first time! We were truly happy. We put so much effort into reaching this moment.

I took the car seat out of the car with Natalie, and once we unpacked all the bags, I lifted her in my arms and said to her, "This is your home now, you can feel safe here."

The End

Our daughter Natalie

Addendum

Our greatest glory is not in never falling, but in rising every time we fall.

Confucius

After returning home, it wasn't easy. My wife and I shared the responsibilities. Less than a month later, we drove to my mom's in Belfast for Christmas. It was a wonderful adventure, especially for Natalie, as it was her first Christmas. Sebastian, on the other hand, enjoyed the ferry crossing we took in Scotland. The crossing lasted less than an hour, and the child loved how the ferry swayed on the sea waves.

We spent the entire vacation very pleasantly in the beautiful city of Belfast. We visited most of the tourist attractions, and two days after New Year's Eve, we returned home.

The little one slowly began to grow and develop. Considering the condition she was in, it is truly an incredible story.

Almost four years have passed since the events described in this book. Everything was going well until February of the year 2022 when Natalie's older brother was diagnosed with Acute Lymphoblastic Leukemia.

A new battle for the child's life commenced, this time centered around Sebastian.

Paul Mikulicz

The author of the book and the father of the main character is me - Paul. In my daily life, I am a loving husband, father, sports enthusiast, and traveler. I arrived in the United Kingdom in 2011, where I met my wife Eve, and started a family. My greatest sporting achievement is completing a double Trifecta in the Spartan Race, which involves running six obstacle races totaling approximately 72 kilometers in one year. On the other hand, my biggest dream is to win a medal in the Spartan Ultra Beast race and stand on the podium. I would also like to write more books to be able to share with other parents who are dealing with similar illnesses in their children, so they never give up in the fight for their children's health and strive for it with all their might, without urging them.

All the quotes used in the text were transcribed from the internet